The
SWING
FACTORY

First published in Great Britain by Simon & Schuster UK Ltd, 2004
A Viacom company

Art direction and design by Jeremy Butcher and Fiona Andreanelli
Illustrations by Kevin Tweddell c/o Artists Partners
All photographs, except those listed below, © Charles Briscoe-Knight, and © Eric Hepworth
p. 31 Richard Branson © Rex Features
p.26 Michael Bonallack © Associated Sports Photography
p.17, p.19, p.21, p.22, p.23, p.24, p.25, p.30 courtesy of The Knightsbridge Golf School

3 5 7 9 10 8 6 4

Simon & Schuster UK Ltd
Africa House
64–78 Kingsway
London WC2B 6AH

www.simonsays.co.uk

Simon & Schuster Sydney Australia

A CIP catalogue record for this book is available from the British Library

ISBN 0 7432 5256 X

Printed and bound in Great Britain, by The Bath Press, Bath.

The SWING FACTORY

William Sieghart
Steve Gould
D.J. Wilkinson

LONDON SYDNEY NEW YORK TORONTO

With thanks to Charles Briscoe-Knight, Jeremy Butcher, Fiona Andreanelli, Melissa Weatherill, Arianne Burnette, Ian Chapman, Ed Victor, Felicity Ann Sieghart, Molly Dineen, Hugh Grant, Christopher Lee, DJ Spoony, Glenn Collins, Alan Lacey, Nicki Rule, Joshua White, Darrell Bennett, William Scott and Daniel Wolf.

Dedicated to Leslie King, the master of the modern swing

contents

'It don't mean a thing
if it ain't got that swing'

Duke Ellington

introduction

The Swing Factory: an introduction

A few years ago, inspired by a friend to make an unscheduled visit to a driving range in the mountains of Colorado, I took up golf. The high altitude meant that the ball would fly improbable distances the few times that I struck it well and instantly I began to fall in love with the game. Little by little I began to get better at it, but after a while I realised I had reached the limit of my abilities and began to have some lessons here and there. Various professionals made adjustments to different parts of my grip, address or swing and for a short while I felt I was still improving.

Somehow or other, though, I was trapped in a cycle. I would have my good days and bad days on the course. And if the day started badly, more often than not it would get worse. As I became more frustrated, my swing became more disjointed. Most important of all, when things went wrong, I didn't know what to do or how to correct it. After a few bad swings I would become defeatist and defeated. And as any keen golfer will tell you, when you are caught up in this cycle of desperation, there is nothing worse.

I was explaining this to an elderly New Yorker one day and she smiled, reached into her handbag for a pen and paper, wrote down a name and number and told me that salvation was on the way.

Of course I didn't believe her and the scrap of paper stayed on my desk for months before one painful day, when my battle with the game had reached a new and extreme low, I decided to book myself a lesson.

Suffice it to say that not only did my experience at the Swing Factory help me escape this painful cycle, but it also resulted in me writing this book. When I first entered the Factory, my handicap would have been a charitable 24. Just over twelve months later, I was competing in the Dunhill Cup, a pro-am tournament played on some of the greatest and most famous courses in Scotland. On the first day of the tournament, on the Old Course at St Andrews, the home of the game of golf, I hit an 81, a mere 9 over par, a score that I had dreamt about many times but never believed possible for me to achieve. It was as though I had discovered golf's Holy Grail.

On the first day of the tournament, on the Old Course at St Andrews, the home of the game of golf, I hit an 81, a mere 9 over par, a score that I had dreamt about many times but never believed possible for me to achieve. It was as though I had discovered golf's Holy Grail.

Golf's best-kept secret

'That some achieve success is proof that all others can achieve it as well' ABRAHAM LINCOLN

47, Lowndes Square, London, home of the Swing Factory.

and his two professionals, D. J. Wilkinson and Steve Gould, the co-authors of this book, have taught the secret to tens of thousands of pupils, turning complete beginners into single handicap golfers and budding professionals into winners of major tournaments. Their school alumni include an extraordinary list of world-class professionals, national and county amateur champions and some of the great golfing celebrities of our time.

What makes the Swing Factory's teachings so different is that you can learn them at home or in the garden – all you need is enough space to swing a club. This is because the focus of the method is on perfecting your swing before you learn to strike the ball. Mastering the principles and practising the exercises in this book for five minutes a day will give you the foundations of a consistent swing and a familiarity with the feel of a golf club that will pay enormous dividends.

This book is about golf's best-kept secret. Over the last sixty years it has helped countless amateur and professional golfers to transform their golf games. They learned the secret from Leslie King, the most influential golf teacher of the last half of the twentieth century, and the inventor of the first-ever modern golf method. During his sixty-year teaching career, Leslie King

Swing Factory professionals Steve Gould and D. J. Wilkinson.

A poster advertising Leslie King's golf column, which he wrote in London's *Evening News* in the early 1970s.

Instead of hoping to have a good day on the course, you'll feel confident as you stand over the ball on the first tee.

Most golfers have the same problem: time. It takes hours to play a round of golf, and by the time you've got to the golf course and back, much of the day has gone. You only have to visit a driving range to see that most golfers are not benefiting from the time they put aside to practise because they are merely reinforcing their swing faults and not getting any better at the game. For the vast majority of golfers, it is impossible to improve their golf or to play more consistently. The Swing Factory shows you how you can do both, without having to go anywhere to do it.

If you follow the Swing Factory's teaching method in this book, your handicap will be dramatically lowered and you will have the fundamentals of a great golf swing for years to come. Rest assured the method works for anyone, whether you are a beginner or an experienced golfer, or whether you are five or eighty-five years old.

The history of the Swing Factory

The story of Leslie King and his method –
His pupils from Gary Player to Juli Inkster –
King's legacy to the modern game

'Start by doing what's necessary, then what's
possible, and suddenly you are doing the
impossible' St Francis of Assisi

The story of the Swing Factory begins in the 1920s and 1930s, when the game of golf was not as accessible to millions of people as it is today. This was partly because golf tuition was in its infancy. Beginners learned to play golf by copying the swing of others and only visited the professional at their golf club to cure a hook, a top or a slice or to correct their self-taught swing.

The greatest players of the day were the most naturally gifted golfers who acquired their skills through emulating others and a rigorous routine of practice. Only those with strong imitative instincts could prosper, because there was no theory of the golf swing and therefore no fundamental system of learning. Talented golfers had no way of passing on their skills to others. Those who could play well only did so because of their natural gifts. They found the game relatively simple to master. But for the majority of players who were not blessed with these natural skills, the game was very hard indeed.

As always in sport, the leading players of that era were the icons of their age. Players such as Harry Vardon, James Braid and J. H. Taylor inspired the golfing public, and thousands of enthusiasts would follow them around the golf course. They were the players with the most beautiful swings of all and many of the naturally gifted golfers of the day learned to play by watching them.

This tradition of learning the game by mimicking the masters can be traced back through the golfing generations to the latter part of the nineteenth century, when the passion for the game of golf began to spread from Scotland across the British Isles and into the United States through successive waves of Scottish emigration. Hundreds of golf courses were constructed on

Leslie King teaching his method in the Knightsbridge Golf School in 1954. His pupil is Helen Jean Banbury, a single-figure handicapper who still visits today.

both sides of the Atlantic, mostly designed by the great Scottish golfers of the time, and thousands of enthusiasts queued up to learn and play the game.

Despite this explosion of interest, it wasn't until Leslie King started to develop his ideas in the late 1920s that the beginnings of the first theory and method of teaching the swing appeared on the golfing scene. As an aspiring young club professional, King wanted to move on from the imitative tradition of learning and teaching golf, and decided to apply a more principled form of analysis to the golf swing. For five years he followed the greatest golfers of his age around the course, sometimes travelling hundreds of miles on an old motorbike to watch them play on his days off from work. Without the modern aid of videotape or video cameras to help him, he had to rely on his quick eyes and his extremely sharp analytical mind. In particular, he followed Vardon and Taylor, the two greatest golfers of the era, as well as the most talented visiting Americans, when they began to come over to compete in the British Open.

After five years of careful research, King defined what he called 'the basic model of the golf swing and its defining principles'. From his research, he believed that he knew everything there was to know about what was happening technically in the swing. What he had learned were the principles behind each movement in the great players' swings. Even though each player's swing looked and seemed different, the defining principles remained the same. The essential parts never varied; he coupled this knowledge with a more scientific understanding of the underlying forces that produced a powerful and accurate delivery of the club-head to the golf ball and that

sustained the club-head through the arc of the swing. To develop his model for teaching King took in every detail of every movement in each of the great players' swings. He watched the arc of the club in its entirety. He noted every movement of the head, the hands, the arms and the shoulders. Even the fingers didn't escape his attention. He noted the rotation of the hips, the flex of the knees and the position of the players' feet and toes. Nothing escaped him.

At around the same time, a number of golf professionals in the United States were beginning to write about the concept of centrifugal force as the main source of power in the swing; the driving force, so to speak, of the golf swing. King built on this theory to develop his method. The concept is best understood by a simple demonstration, which you can try at home, known by Leslie King as 'feeling the force'.

Find a shaft of a club unattached to a club-head. You can usually borrow one from a pro shop, but if you cannot find one, a piece of bamboo or something with similarly whippy qualities will do. Take it in one hand and grip it as if it were a golf club. Draw the shaft back as though you were going to make a one-handed backswing. Then lash the shaft through to a finished follow-through. You will hear the shaft zip through the air and you will 'feel the force' that flows from the body through the shoulder and then through the arm, wrist and hand up through the club-shaft with extraordinary speed and power.

Now try the same process while holding the club-shaft with your other hand. This exercise will give you an idea of the potential power you have in your golf swing when you have really got the swing shape right.

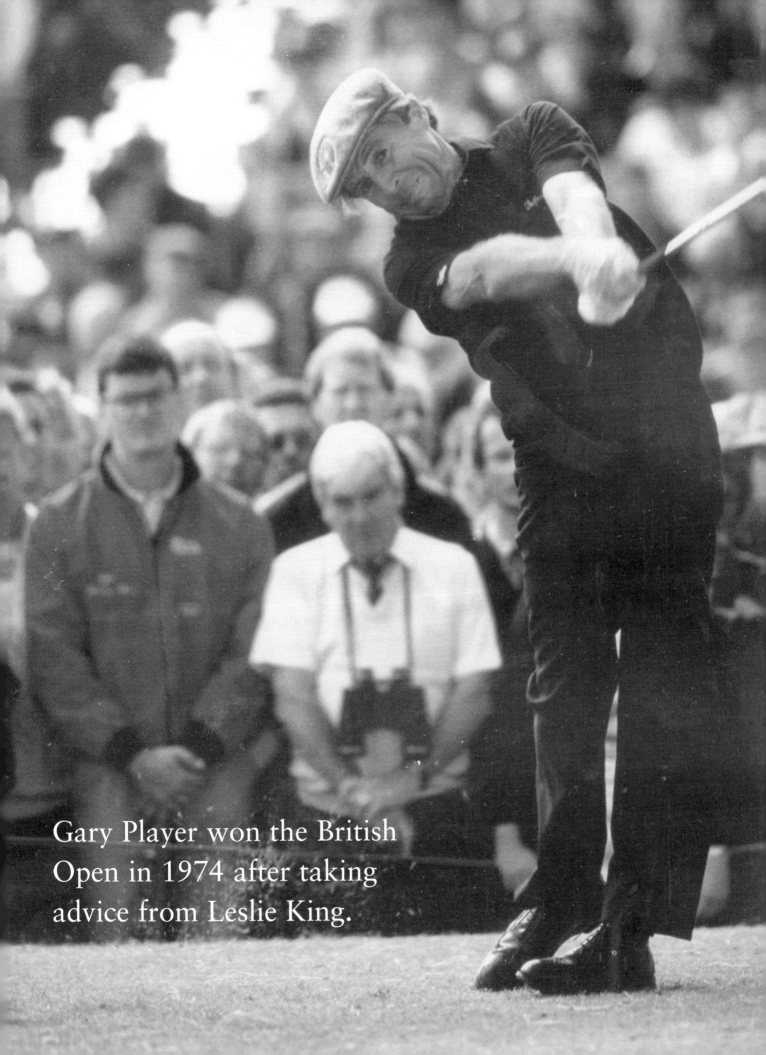

Gary Player won the British Open in 1974 after taking advice from Leslie King.

As well as watching the players' movements, King concentrated on the movements of the club-shaft and the club-face, not just at the point of impact but also at each and every point in the swing. All this he took in at a glance, in the time it takes to swing a golf club. His eyes were so sharp that if a club moved in a player's hands he could see it. He could even see from which part of the club-face the player hit the ball. He could tell if the club-face was open, closed or straight at any part of the swing. He would watch the line of the club through the ball and he could tell the height and direction of each shot just by seeing the swing. He never needed to look where the ball went. The swing path and power of the swing told him everything.

Players' swings also told him how much punishment their body was taking. King could even tell where in the player's body the swing would hurt, whether in the back, elbow, wrist or even thumbs. Nothing was overlooked. Years later Michael Bonallack, one of the greatest amateur golfers of the century, would have his persistent back problems cured by reshaping his swing under the careful eye of Leslie King. He also went on to win five British Amateur Championships.

King's knowledge now had depth and precision. He got himself a job as a professional at the Malden Golf Club in Surrey. His teaching reputation preceded him and he gave lessons from early in the morning until the sun began to set. In time his club employers began to get impatient. He seemed to have no time for the other duties of a resident golf professional – selling green fees, equipment and mending golf clubs – because the demands on his time as a teacher were so great. Eventually King left Malden to set up the Knightsbridge Golf School in

a basement squash court in London, where it still thrives and prospers today under the tutelage of this book's co-authors, his two professionals, D. J. Wilkinson and Steve Gould.

King had set up indoors because he no longer needed to see the golf ball fly. The swing told him everything he needed to know. To his surprise, he also found that his pupils improved more quickly by learning indoors than they had done outdoors. It rapidly became clear to him that his pupils could focus a lot better on each specific part of the swing if they weren't worried about where the ball was going. The indoor teaching environment also made a difference. It was easier to concentrate in warm, dry conditions than on a cold, wet and windy practice ground.

King's assessment of his pupils was exacting. When working with a pupil with serious professional or amateur ambitions, he would begin by taking his or her physique into account. Having made his initial assessment, he would then turn to the pupil's posture: how straight or rounded the spine was, how wide or narrow the

James Bond plays against Goldfinger in cinema's most famous round of golf. Sean Connery was one of Leslie King's most famous pupils.

chest and how long or short the projection of the neck. From this subtle picture King would create exercises with and without a club to tailor-make a swing that would develop and accommodate the player's build.

Whenever possible he would change a player's physique to improve his or her swing. It was not unusual for visitors to the studio to see a pupil, male or female, doing press-ups in the middle of a lesson. Hands were strengthened, spines straightened and chests expanded. On one famous occasion a player who went on to become a successful professional was put through a painful series of neck-lengthening exercises.

Once a pupil's physical abilities had been determined, then corrected and improved as far as possible, he or she would work on acquiring the swing shape by absorbing each part of its structure with great precision. Pupils had to learn how to stop at any point in their swing and check the shape for themselves. This meant that they became their own teacher and instructor. And as you will learn from this book, once you have acquired the shape of your swing, the movements gradually blend together, evolving naturally.

King would make his pupils practise in slow motion and then begin to add the centrifugal force that would bring power into the swing.

Three successive US amateur titles and many professional major tournament wins were Juli Inkster's reward for working with Leslie King.

This would transform the swing into a free-flowing entity. Even at half speed he taught his pupils to acquire the feeling of centrifugal force. This meant they were now able to acquire the greatest possible power that their own strength and coordination allowed, turning the finished product into a stylish natural swing.

King also assessed each pupil's mind and aptitude to learning the game. He wanted to look into the pupils' minds to understand the way in which they thought and to use their natural mental attributes to help them learn. Some pupils had what he called a practical mind with good coordination, rhythm and the ability to mimic. He would set about teaching these pupils in an imitative way. But the majority of pupils learned through their intellect so that each and every detail had to be explained and understood.

King used what modern psychologists would call the cognitive process to help his pupils absorb his teachings. With most students he combined elements of the cognitive and the imitative, but a few of his pupils found it difficult to learn either way. They were, to use the modern term, dyspraxic, and struggled to pick up on his teaching. King developed a method for them to learn by holding their arms and making the swing for them. By having every movement physically shaped for them, they were able to absorb his method by feeling and to reproduce the movements without him.

King also divided his pupils into different types depending on their levels of concentration. Some had what he called 'a one-dimensional mind', totally focused in a cocoon of concentration, oblivious to any distractions. Other pupils had 'a multi-tasking mind' and were more easily distracted by other thoughts. They were more likely to be thinking about the phone call they hadn't made or had left half their mind in the office or would be worrying about some business deal halfway through their downswing. The final group of his pupils were those who, like Lee Trevino, could switch their mind from one topic to another without it affecting their concentration. Trevino was a player who could talk and talk and then switch in a moment to perfect concentration on his shot.

King's belief was that the conscious mind is the golfer's biggest enemy – a proposition all golfers will understand.

Most of his pupils were highly successful business people in their own right who brought a focused mind to the task. They expected success, they had a good work ethic, and they knew what it took to be successful at anything. They were prepared to work and then work harder. They were not easily deterred by failure. But the work they did had to be absolutely clearly defined and understood. As all learners will tell you, it is no good working in a vacuum with no point of reference. With King they always had a crystal clear understanding of what was required with a perfect blueprint to follow. As a result they enjoyed the learning process.

King's belief was that the conscious mind is the golfer's biggest enemy – a proposition all golfers will understand. Once the swing had been built

into a pupil's subconscious, the conscious mind must be retrained or it will interfere with the natural free movement and distort the pure swing. Conscious attempts to swing are what trigger the wrong reflexes and destroy timing.

A player's individual golf history will add to potential complications by bringing the old bad habits retained by the subconscious into conflict with and degrading the new swing. In time the subconscious will acquire the new structure and that structure will be mostly dominant, but under extreme pressure what is first learned by the subconscious tends to be reproduced.

The history of your shot-making, as any golfer knows, is in the mind. Success or failure is wrapped up in the history of your experience. What lies ahead for you is in your imagination and your imagination is influenced by your past experience. Preparation, therefore, is everything, however well prepared you are; even preparation is only part of the solution when the test comes. The enigma of all things in life lies in the

Three of Leslie King's pupils win national amateur titles on the same day in the 1970s.

Steve Gould and D. J. Wilkinson with Stephen Ames after he won the 1996 Benson and Hedges International.

unknown and how you deal with it. Often luck or good fortune will play its part, but preparing well will give you the best chance of success.

By combining the principles of his swing theory with his pupils' physical and mental characteristics, King was able to hand on to them the gifts of the natural golfers he had followed through his years of learning. Their personal oddities and mannerisms were ignored and discounted. King had found the lowest common denominator of the swing and, based on this understanding, had begun to build beautiful and simple swings for his clients. The results were spectacular.

Not only did King's existing pupils from Malden follow him to Knightsbridge, but the glitterati of the era began to come too. Rock stars and big names in show business, newspaper tycoons and politicians, entrepreneurs and city folk, intellectuals and scientists, even taxi drivers, filled the studio eager to learn from the modern master.

After a lifetime of teaching, King's whole process of analysis had become instinctive and almost

subconscious. He could tell from a swing or two and a quick glance at a player's physique exactly what was required to turn him or her into a champion. He would share with the players his vision of what they could achieve and if they were willing to work with him he would pursue it with them with a relentless passion.

Like many of the most successful coaches in sport King was a hard taskmaster, but the photographs of trophy winners on the wall were enough to convince even the most reluctant and doubtful. Here was the route to golfing success. King was an inspired and inspiring teacher. His enthusiasm was infectious and his catchphrase famous: 'there is nothing you can do that I don't see. I even know what you are thinking.' To his many pupils it always felt like he did.

Rock stars and big names in show business, newspaper tycoons and politicians, entrepreneurs and city folk, intellectuals and scientists, even taxi drivers, filled the studio eager to learn from the modern master.

In 1953 King was struck down by cancer. Despite the fact that he was undergoing overwhelming doses of radiotherapy, he continued to drag himself into the school to give lessons. Luckily his treatment worked and he was able to continue teaching until the age of eighty-four. He died, aged eighty-seven, in 1995.

Sean Connery shows off his Swing Factory finish in the film *Goldfinger*.

Michael Bonallack, five times British Amateur Champion, studied under Leslie King.

Leslie King was one of the old school, a man who had been brought up in the early years of the twentieth century, when life was much harder than it is today. He went to work when he was nine years old, scrubbing kitchen floors before he went to school. Injured and invalided out of the army after the Second World War, he lost the use of his legs and was unable to walk for two whole years. He had dragged a pilot out of a burning plane. Not only did he manage to overcome his physical disabilities, but his extraordinary sense of purpose also sent him into an intensely physical occupation. The result of his inquiries, after looking into the heart of a subject that was complex and difficult to fathom, was to find a beautiful and simple explanation.

One of King's great legacies to the game of golf was that, apart from his teaching method, he established the proper separation between the playing professional and the teaching professional. These are completely different roles that require very different skills. When you look at the top names in golf coaching, men such as Butch Harmon and David Leadbetter, you will notice that neither has had a particularly distinguished professional playing career nor is either of them attached to a golf club with its concomitant responsibilities.

The evolution of the teaching professional as a distinct career and the science of golf instruction have been slow, but it is no accident

It is no accident that many of the current breed of successful teachers, including David Leadbetter, passed through Leslie King's studio at some stage in their professional development.

that many of the current breed of successful teachers, including David Leadbetter, passed through Leslie King's studio at some stage in their professional development.

King's legacy can be seen across the professional tour on both sides of the Atlantic. Some years back Nick Faldo became famous for making the decision to rebuild his swing, recognising its potential fragility. He chose Leadbetter as his teacher. Faldo was a classic example of the naturally gifted golfer who had learned his golfing skills imitatively. In his time rebuilding his swing, he learned where to be at each point in it, giving the swing the strength to withstand the ravages of confidence and competition.

These days, thanks to the lasting influence of King's methods on modern teaching, the shape of most golfers' swings look alike. Most professionals with a history of long-term success in the game have worked on developing their swing knowledge in a similar way. It has proved very hard for professionals to remain consistently successful over a period of years without the strength of such a method behind them. Those who don't have it can often have a meteoric rise on the back of their extraordinary natural gifts but find the challenge of maintaining their success impossible.

For the professional golfer, the margins of error between success and failure can be minuscule. Their swings are balanced on a knife-edge. Some high quality players reach the pinnacle of the game only to fall away. Players such as Sandy Lyle and Seve Ballesteros never seemed to recover the talents of their youth. Even the most consistent of them all, Colin Montgomerie, is finding a few problems, at the time of writing, with a game that had seemed so simple. And the

most talented golfer of the last hundred years, Tiger Woods, continues to struggle with his driver from the tee. No swing is perfect by definition. That is why having a method behind your swing is so important.

By the end of his teaching career, King had taught three or four generations of the same families how to play golf. Some of his pupils were as old as eighty-five, others as young as three years old. He legendarily prepared Sean Connery for his famous round of golf in the film *Goldfinger*. Juli Inkster, one of the greatest ever women golfers, a record winner of three successive US Amateur Championships and a winner of many Majors, made an annual pilgrimage from the US for lessons.

An extraordinary flow of champions, who won countless professional, national amateur and county championships, came out of King's basement studio and his reputation spread far afield. As well as Inkster, a succession of top players from the United States started to fly in to London for instruction. Bob Toski, one of America's greatest teachers, who had described Leslie King as the 'godfather of the modern golf swing', flew over to meet King and to study his method at close hand. Gary Player won the British Open in 1974 after taking tips from Leslie King.

Today the school's profile continues to rise. Its professional pupils regularly win tournaments and its appointment books are permanently full. The school's client list over the last few years reads like a showbiz *Who's Who*. Hugh Grant, Bryan Ferry, Christopher Lee, Diana Rigg, Telly Savalas, Richard Branson, Kyle Maclachlan, Michael Flatley and Gianfranco Zola, to name but a few, have all been regular visitors.

Steve Gould
Knightsbridge School of Golf
47 Lowndes Square
London
SW1X 9YU

Dear Steve,

I just wanted to drop you a note to thank you and Dave for all the help you've given my father and me. It is hard to say which of us came to you the worse golfer, but you have done the impossible and turned us from embarrassing into respectable.

We've both tried a number of other teachers over the years, but none have ever come close to achieving what you have. Just like Mrs Banfield at my primary school, you can be strict, but it's for our own good, and the results have certainly been well worth it. (And <u>you</u> never hit me with a ruler – or at least only that once, and I deserved it).

So many, many thanks. As they say in America – you guys are the best.

Hugh Grant.

'Leslie King's teachings
helped me win three
consecutive US Amateur
Championships. In later
years I continued flying
over to England especially
for lessons with Steve and
Dave. I went on to win
two US Opens and have
been elected to golf's Hall
of Fame. I will always be
grateful for the teachings
of Leslie King.'

I've been a Swing Factory regular for nearly forty years,
and after my last visit when 73, to see championship golf
courses I have always before wanting I thoroughly recommend
the teachings of the Swing Factory.

'The Swing Factory has
given me the foundations
for what I believe will be a
lifetime's enjoyable golf.'
DJ Spawn

'I sent my mum to the Swing
Factory for a series of lessons
that changed her life. I can't
thank the Swing Factory
enough for helping her get so
much enjoyment from the
game she loves.' Roger Freeman

'I didn't take up golf until I was
thirty, and found that for years I
made no progress. I was confused
by all the different advice I was
given and felt I had no time to
make any significant improvement.
Thankfully I was introduced to the
Swing Factory and had instant
success.' Lord Derby Vice President

From beginner to believer

'To see a world in a grain of sand, and a heaven in a wild flower, hold infinity in the palm of your hand, and eternity in an hour' WILLIAM BLAKE

The most frustrating part about playing golf before I first visited the Swing Factory was that I didn't really know what I was doing. When I hit a good shot I didn't know why and when I hit a bad shot I didn't know why either. I had no method of correcting my faults once I was out on the course. The only potential rescue from that total sense of despondency when things went completely wrong was a lesson. And a lesson, if I did have time for one, only ever gave me a quick and fleeting fix. This was frustrating because there are few things in life that give such acute aesthetic satisfaction as a beautifully hit golf ball.

I think this is the reason why more people seem to be hooked on golf than any other game. Even people who know nothing about the game and never play it are addicted to watching it on television. It is envy-inducing the ease with which the great golfers strike the ball, sending it soaring into the air, purely and cleanly.

It is partly the pleasure of watching people display such precise skills, the delicacy of their sense of touch and the grace of their movement. Just as it is entertaining to see a nippy winger beat his man at soccer or a gymnast execute a tricky tumble. But the game of golf has an extra

dimension. For it is not just the physical attributes of the game that grip the participants and the spectators, it is also the psychological.

The psychological journey that every player goes through during a round of golf is what makes the sport so complex and uniquely addictive. No other game has so many psychological difficulties to deal with because in golf you are playing against yourself. There is a succession of problems to get your mind around: your score – the card in your pocket that you don't dare add up when things are going well, your swing, and thoughts of hazards up ahead and what might go wrong, and the myriad mental distractions that three or four hours of walking around a golf course can bring to you.

Many people find that golf represents more than just a game in their lives. They use it as a diversionary activity to resolve problems. The process of calming the mind and, if you are lucky, mastering both the course and your opponent can be deeply therapeutic. The time and space that a round of golf allows in our increasingly frenetic lives can often provide resolution to all kinds of issues hovering in the subconscious. For me, on the occasions that I play a really good round,

The teachings that are contained in this book gave me a discipline. They taught me where to be at each point in the swing and how to correct things when they went wrong.

The resounding message of this book is that 95 per cent of golfers share 95 per cent of the same faults. Day after day, week after week, month after month, year after year, visitors to the Swing Factory bring with them exactly the same errors in their swing.

exceeding my own expectations, it provides me with more pleasure than almost anything I do.

What is it about the relationship between man and ball that makes ball games so seductive? Why will a child happily play with a ball for hours and hours on end? Through the years a ball has been a thing of great comfort to me, a companion in times of need. It got me through many bad patches in my childhood. After hours spent playing with a ball it seemed almost to become a part of me, an extension of my own physical being. Once I mastered the mechanics of kicking a football or hitting a tennis ball, I could then begin to manipulate it, bend it, swerve it or spin it. And working on these ball skills became an endlessly fulfilling challenge in itself.

Most ball games are relatively easy to play compared to golf. To get a good contact with a football or tennis ball isn't hard. Both the ball and the tennis racket are reasonably sized. But golf laughs at us. It looks easy to hit a stationary ball yet it isn't. The ball and the club-face are very small and the margin of error is even smaller.

This is why to play golf well, unlike many other ball games, you need a method. You cannot rely on good hand-to-eye coordination alone. Technique is everything and there are no short cuts. This is where the Swing Factory comes in. The teachings that are contained in this book gave me a discipline. They taught me where to be at each point in the swing and how to correct things when they went wrong. Now if I start to hook or slice or hit the ground first, or display any of the many faults that all golfers will recognise, I can cure it there and then before I repeat my mistake.

Most important of all, by being able to rely on my technique, my confidence doesn't completely collapse after I make a mistake or even a series of mistakes. This means that I no longer plunge into the depths of despair, which can be so humiliating and depressing to live with, and at last I have a secure and stable foundation for my game.

This book has not been written by a world-famous touring professional. Unfortunately, those books that are written by professionals often aren't very helpful to the average golfer. Their instructional books and videos are about them and how they play the game.

By contrast, this book is written in the certain knowledge that its contents can transform the average golfer into a good golfer. And if, sadly, like many golfers, the quality of your golf has become a barometer for your life, that can only be a good thing.

The resounding message of this book is that 95 per cent of golfers share 95 per cent of the same faults. Day after day, week after week, month after month, year after year, visitors to the Swing Factory bring with them exactly the same errors in their swings.

So this book is dedicated to the average golfer, to anyone who has struggled to master a game that has brought much joy to many and much misery to many, many more. Whether you are a seasoned player or a beginner, it will be invaluable. It contains the only instruction you will ever need to build a solid, repeatable golf swing.

The golfer's journey
Why you need a plan – Finding the zone

'Our greatest battles are those with our minds'
JAMESON FRANK

A good golf swing should be performed subconsciously. It should have smoothness and tempo. It should be as fluid and natural as a bird in flight. To the player or the spectator the swing should be a thing of beauty and, above all, it should be beautifully simple. So the good golfer should not hack. He should not heave. He should be in harmony with his swing.

If you are able to learn golf by imitation at an early age, you may be able to play with this sense of harmony for the rest of your life. Every week on the television you see professionals who started playing golf as children picking up a million dollars in prize money. For the rest of us who are not Tiger Woods or one of the chosen ones on the professional tour, golf is not like this. For us golf is difficult and, as golf's journeymen, in order to play well, we have to devise a plan to achieve a beautiful swing through conscious thought.

Herein lies the problem. The conscious mind of an adult is not very well adapted to such a task. You only have to look along the driving range to realise that the 'ascent of man' stops here. Most golfers are playing hit-and-hope golf. They just try to hit the ball and hope it goes in the desired direction.

The purpose of this book is to release you from hit-and-hope golf by teaching you how to understand every inch of your swing and where you should be at every point in it. It will teach you how to find the four main positions in the swing and how to move from each point to the next. By consciously finding and checking these positions, you will begin to acquire the correct shape to your swing. Then, by blending the movements together in slow motion, you will begin to link the parts together smoothly. Constant repetition of these movements makes them become part of your subconscious rather like when you are changing gears in a car.

Once you can programme your mind to repeat the swing subconsciously, then it takes very little conscious thought to achieve a good swing. Your mind becomes free to focus on striking the ball to the target and on any subtle variations of the shot that you are trying to make. No amount of mental strength or desire is a substitute for sound technique. The closer you come to technical perfection, the better the mind can function, freed of the distractions of worrying about the swing. And this breeds – the critical word in golf – confidence.

In golf, the hardest thing to do is to control your mind. It knows how bad or good you really are at the game, so you have to have the inbuilt technical confidence to focus your mind on the good player in you and not the bad.

Once you have that confidence and the correct movements of the swing have become engrained into your subconscious, you have the potential to move into what golfers call the 'zone'.

Confidence comes from sound technique. Sound technique produces good shots. The good shots inspire more confidence and confidence removes fear. Conversely, bad shots will undermine your confidence. The more destructive the bad shot, the worse the loss of confidence. As any golfer knows, the more often you repeat the bad shot, the more tense and frightened you become. Under pressure you will often repeat your worst shots.

In golf, the hardest thing to do is to control your mind. It knows how bad or good you really are at the game, so you have to have the inbuilt technical confidence to focus your mind on the good player in you and not the bad.

Once you have that confidence and the correct movements of the swing have become engrained into your subconscious, you have the potential to move into what golfers call the 'zone'. The zone is the ultimate goal of the golfer and is achieved when the body obeys the mind's commands and every complex muscle movement in the golf swing is produced in the right order at the right time without the need for conscious thought.

This means that the old enemies in your swing have been temporarily defeated or subdued. You feel you are in a place where mind and body seem to be in perfect harmony. Great players have described it as a state of heightened awareness through which their golf game reaches the pinnacle of perfection.

When you can capture this exalted state, which is possible for even ordinary players for parts of a round, when shot after shot after shot flies from the middle of the club-face towards the target, here at last, for a moment or even for an hour, the marriage of mind and matter is complete. The perfection of golf is within your grasp.

But, like all moments of perfection in this life, they don't go on forever. Slowly the mind resumes its old habits and conscious thought begins to interfere with your game. The magic is lost and you begin to stumble. The body, no longer under control of the mind, rebels. Reflexes start to trigger too early, chaos ensues and disaster follows. This is where the work of the conscious mind has to begin again to draw you back to the 'plan', back to thinking about how you can reconnect to the subconscious ease of your swing and not let conscious anger get in the way.

This psychological journey that one goes through during a round of golf is the central problem of the game, since the desire to overcome yourself as your own worst enemy afflicts every player from the highest to the lowest. Even Tiger Woods, with the world at his feet, continues in this personal struggle to beat his demons in every round that he plays.

Do you recognise this golfing journey? You are now about to learn a method that will help you deal with it for the rest of your golfing career.

'Nothing is particularly hard if you divide it into small jobs'

<small>HENRY FORD</small>

how it works

How it works

The Swing Factory's method teaches you how to build your swing in four easy stages, with exercises to help you do it. None of these require a golf ball to begin with. Once you've mastered the basics, you can practise out on the range or the course. All you need is enough space to swing a golf club.

To begin with, you should move through the four swing stages in slow motion, checking every detail as you go along. This is very important. Don't try to rush from one position to the next. After a while you will find that your swing will become more natural and fluid, but as you put it together you must take the utmost care in linking the stages, as though you are joining the dots.

There are illustrations and photographs to help you, but if you have access to a digital or video camera and a full-length mirror, you will find them immensely helpful. With most modern video equipment, you can watch your swing frame by frame and compare it to the pictures in this book. A large mirror will enable you to see yourself in action as you learn the stages of the full swing. There are two different illustrated views to guide you through the swing. The first is from behind and slightly to the right of you if you are right-handed. This is where you should place your video or digital camera to capture your swing. The second is what we call the mirror view, a direct mirror image facing you as you swing.

From behind

This is where you should place the mirror.
The only other equipment you will need are
a golf club – ideally a 5-iron – to swing with
and a rubber mat with a hole in it and a rubber
tee. As well as teaching you how to build a
reliable swing, you'll also learn how to correct
things if they go wrong. Almost all golfers
have the same faults, and most adopt
a trial-and-error approach to curing
them. But you will find that the Swing Factory
method teaches you a systematic way of curing
your swing faults there and then.

For those of you who are already golfers, the
Swing Factory may require you to unlearn a few
things. This will take some time and there will
be moments when you may find yourself lost
between your old swing and your new one.
Don't be tempted. The method works and has
worked for tens of thousands of golfers through
the years. And it is the same method for
everyone, young or old.

Most people find the method easy to learn, but
learning anything new can be hard. The older
we get in life, the harder it seems to be to learn new
things – not necessarily because it is actually harder
but often because we have got out of the habit of
learning. Also you might have an inbuilt resistance
to learning and a tendency at times to give up too
easily, believing that you just can't do it.

Certainly, for me, part of the journey of learning
how to swing was also about learning how to
learn again, as well as having to unlearn a few
things. Just as getting round a golf course forces

The mirror view

you to confront your inner demons, so too can the process of learning the swing. To begin with, I was hampered by my past. I was already technically doing all the wrong things: grip, takeaway, finish, the works. Despite this, I was able to get round a golf course in less than 95 strokes.

For the first few weeks of learning at the Swing Factory, I was, as they say in golf, between swings. In other words, while I was learning my new way of swinging, I would find myself bringing in the bad habits of the old. Sometimes if I really couldn't do it the new way, I would return to my old way of playing, a sure-fire recipe for disaster. It is also worth taking the time to get the swing right before you play again rather than absorbing part of the method and then trying it out on the course.

Once you have got the basics right, the simplest way of retaining them is to practise your swing for five minutes a day. Just staying familiar with the feeling of a golf club in your hands and your grooved swing gives you a terrific feeling of confidence when you go out to play.

Be patient, stick to the simple exercises in this book and it will pay great dividends. Similarly, don't tinker with your swing, picking up tips from magazines or other players. More often than not, it is this tinkering that puts the golfer's swing out of its groove. First things first: get your swing shape right before trying to hit a ball on the course. Make sure you can consistently repeat the swing again and again. Then you are ready for the game. Imagine you were a tennis player with an unreliable serve or a pool player with an inconsistent cueing

action. It is inconceivable that you would become really good at the game.

Leslie King always liked to point out that in all golf strokes a well-struck ball, from the full tee-shot to a putt, should be 'driven forward'. A golfer shouldn't aim to 'hit', 'flick' or 'slap' the ball. This is because the swing should be a smooth acceleration from the top of the backswing through the ball to the end of the follow-through. 'Driving the ball forward you blend power with control, keeping the club-face on the ball along the intended line of flight of the ball for that vital fraction of time which ensures firm, accurate shot-making.'

Leslie King wouldn't allow his students on to the golf course until they had mastered a consistent swing. To begin with, he would have them practise quarter and half swings in the studio and then practise swinging their hands and arms without a golf club in their hands when they got home. Only when he was confident that they had the basics of a grooved swing would he let them out on the course. This did wonders for their confidence, because by the time they played a round of golf they were already playing at a good level. Many golfers who might find it hard not to play golf while they are learning should consider learning the Swing Factory method during the winter in golf's close season.

Much of what follows has been taken directly from the original instruction works of Leslie King. It has been updated and modernised and, we hope, made as easy to understand and follow as possible. It is as relevant today as it was over fifty years ago.

As well as teaching you how to build a reliable swing, you'll also learn how to correct things if they go wrong. Almost all golfers have the same faults, and most adopt a trial-and-error approach to curing them. But you will find that the Swing Factory method teaches you a systematic way of curing your swing faults there and then.

The four swing stages

Providing your grip and address are sound, there are only four stages or positions of the swing to be mastered. The left illustration of each page shows you how it should look.

The illustrations of how not to do it are on the right. You may recognise yourself in some of them. Throughout the book you will find pictures of both to help you to identify your

Good   Bad

1. The first position: taking your club back away from the ball until it is in the halfway back position.

1. 95 per cent of golfers make the mistake of twisting their hands from the takeaway to the halfway back position.

faults. Once you have learned these four simple positions and the guiding principles behind the swing, the essentials of the swing are in place. But just to reassure you, 95 per cent of players when they first come to the Swing Factory can't find any of these four positions correctly.

By mastering the four positions and linking them together into one free-flowing movement, you will have a model swing that will last you for life.

Good

Bad

2. The second position: completing the backswing to the top of the swing.

2. By twisting their hands in the takeaway, 95 per cent of golfers are out of position at the top of the backswing.

Good   Bad

3. The third position: the correct downswing leads you to the right impact position in which the club-face strikes the ball.

3. A poor downswing has led to an impact position with no movement of the hips towards the target. The player's body is static. This means that there is absolutely no chance of driving the ball forward with power and accuracy.

Good

Bad

4. The fourth position: the correct line through and beyond impact to a three-quarter finish.

4. 95 per cent of players have no idea what should happen during the follow-through. They think of it as an afterthought. Perfecting your follow-through should be a vital part of your technique. This is because faults that occur just after impact will invariably occur just before impact with catastrophic results.

The five swing principles

As well as the four basic swing positions, there are five fundamental swing thoughts that were at the core of Leslie King's teachings and will help you to transform your game. To King they counteracted the most consistent faults that he came across in tuition. Most hack players get the same things wrong either because they have adapted their way of playing golf from other ball sports that they play or because, like most of us, they have misunderstood what is going on when they see someone on the television make a beautiful golf swing.

These swing thoughts are the five swing principles, which you should try to take out on the course with you whenever you play. These have certainly been crucial to my progress and will be to yours. Much of the golf swing is completely counter-intuitive; without these principles to support the technical positions, you will find it much harder to make the method work for you.

1. Think of the golf swing as beginning not when you start your backswing, but at the top of your backswing when you start your downswing.

The backswing is simply a movement of the hands and arms to place the club in the correct position to start the golf swing. If you make the mistake of thinking that the golf swing starts when you take the club-head away from the ball, then you will create an image in your mind of your swing being a pendulum movement backwards and forwards rather than one that starts at the top of your backswing and ends at the top of your follow-through. The reason this is so important is that most golfers fail to accelerate through the ball and complete their swing properly. Learning to start your swing at the top of your backswing will help you to overcome that.

Leslie King liked to use the example of an archer shooting an arrow. When the archer shoots an arrow, he draws back the bowstring with great care and precision, pauses and then in a moment of stillness lets the weight of the string send the arrow accelerating out of the bow. So it should be with a golf swing, the club should accelerate from a standing start through the ball and end with a perfect follow-through. And as any seasoned archer would tell you, the more consistent your tempo, the more accurate you will be.

Dispel the myth of the backswing. Your backswing should be simply a free movement of the hands and the arms to position the golf club in the right place to begin the downswing, the real golf swing.

Forget any ideas in your mind that the backswing is a build-up of power and strength. If you have any other swing thoughts, you are likely to tense your arms and shoulders, stopping you from swinging fluidly.

START

2. Never try to hit the ball. Swing
   through it. Trying to hit the ball
   will almost certainly lead to a
   faulty swing.

3. Make sure you use your body
   correctly in the swing. In the golf
   swing, your body's only job is to
   allow the arms to move back and
   forth through the complete swing.

When you are standing over the ball, your thoughts should not be about aiming to hit the ball but about trying to complete a perfect swing. Executing the swing successfully will take the golf ball the required distance, depending on the loft of the club used.

As soon as you fall into the trap of thinking that the backswing is a build-up of power, you begin to try to hit the ball, tensing your grip and your arms and body, making it impossible to achieve consistent results.

As you swing through the ball, your body should be making room for the arms to pass by so that the body can swing around with them. The most obvious faults in the swings of golfers who visit the Swing Factory come from their arms being unable to complete the full golf swing because their body is in some way obstructing them.

5. You must have a consistent, reliable swing. Without it, you cannot hope to play consistently good golf. The measure of a golfer is not only how good his good shots are but also how bad his bad shots are. If you have a consistent swing, your mistakes won't punish you over much and cost you too many strokes. You are more likely to hit the ball straight but not the full distance rather than hook or slice your ball into deep trouble.

4. You have to complete your swing. Each swing should end with the perfect follow-through. If you think of the top of the backswing as being the start of the golf swing, then you will understand that the follow-through represents at least a third of your swing.

Without a complete follow-through, you are limiting your chances of finding a consistent direction for the ball. You are also likely to limit your chances of accelerating the club-head through the ball if you don't finish your swing.

To make yourself into a good golfer, you require a consistent, repeatable swing. Because the club-face and the ball are relatively small, the margin of error between a good shot and a bad one is very subtle. Until you can swing the club on the same swing plane consistently, playing golf or going to the range won't help you. You will merely magnify the faults in your swing and engrain them in your muscle memory.

The three requirements of a sound golf swing

Most golfers don't know what they are trying to do when they swing a golf club. Without understanding the basic mechanics of the swing, you won't get it right. So before you pick up a club and begin to learn how to swing it, it helps to stand back for a moment and try to understand exactly what the mechanics of the golf swing involve.

Three things must happen in the golf swing in order for it to be effective. Few golfers are aware of them, and even fewer actually achieve them.

1. Line at impact

The club-head must be travelling along the intended line of flight of the ball through the impact area.

2. Square impact

Not only must the club-head swing
'on-line', but it must also be 'square'
or at right angles to the intended line
of flight of the ball through impact
and beyond.

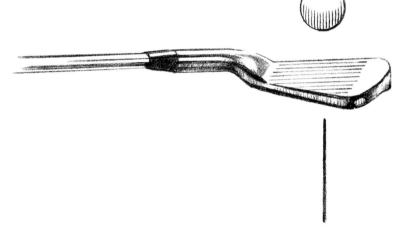

3. Off the middle

The ball must be struck in the
middle of the club-face.

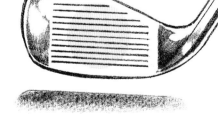

The swing plane

Much of the Swing Factory's method rests on consistently being able to repeat the swing line or swing plane. Look at the illustration and you will see a line going around the golfer's head and following the arc of the club-face through the swing. The club-face is travelling on what we call the swing plane. This book will teach you how to repeat

that swing plane over and over again until you know where your club must be at each point in the swing. The drawing of the plane is not exact. It is to give you an idea of where the club should be. As King put it, 'the good golfer knows exactly where his club must be at any given time, and how to place it there. That's method. Anything else is pure guesswork.'

The section of the swing plane between the feet is called the impact zone. This is the key area. It is what determines the quality of the shot.

Your club-head must be moving squarely along the intended line of flight of the ball before the ball is struck and remain on that line well after impact. The longer the club-head remains on the intended line of flight through impact, the better. Or to put it another way, you should aim to hit the ball for a long time.

This driving forward of the ball is what produces the long, accurate shot that can hold its direction in wind. This is the quality of impact that compresses the golf ball on the club-face almost like a fried egg at the moment of impact. This is the type of impact that leads to powerful, accurate shot-making and low scores.

That is what the golf swing is all about. That is why you must stand square to the intended line of flight of the ball. That is why the swing plane must be properly aligned. You must learn to be

aware of the 'club-line' or the direction that the club-head is taking through the ball.

Never lose sight of this vital concept of the club-line through the ball.

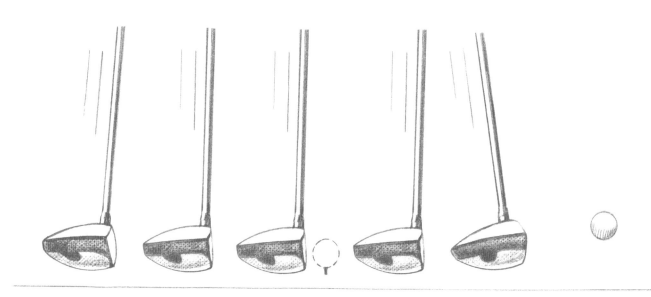

Your club-head must be moving squarely along the intended line of flight of the ball before the ball is struck and remain on that line well after impact. The longer the club-head remains on the intended line of flight through impact, the better. Or to put it another way, you should aim to hit the ball for a long time.

The grip
Part 1 – Left Hand

Perhaps the oldest cliché in golf instruction is that a good grip is the foundation of a sound swing. Every golf book ever written contains a chapter about the grip, with every detail of the grip lavishly illustrated. Unfortunately, what those books don't tell you is what the function of the grip is in the swing. If they did, players would have a better understanding of the importance of the grip, and how to get it right.

Given that the details of the orthodox grip are so well known, why is it that so few golfers actually stick with it? The tragic truth is that few golfers are able to keep to the right golf grip because they have too many errors in their swing actions. Most golfers are consistently changing their grip to try to minimise the errors in their swings. The secret is that they should be rebuilding their swings not their grips.

So get your grip right and stick to it. If you can't play golf with an orthodox grip, it is your swing that needs attention not your grip. You can't cure a bad swing with an equally bad grip.

So what is the role of the grip in the swing? Like every other aspect of the swing, common sense principles govern the orthodox golf grip. In all bat and ball sports, you aim to get the striking surface of the bat or racquet or club moving squarely along the intended line of flight of the ball.

If you can't play golf with an orthodox grip, it is your swing that needs attention not your grip. You can't cure a bad swing with an equally bad grip.

A correct grip simply enables one to swing the club backwards (to the top), and return it to the ball (in the downswing) so that the club-face is both square to the intended line of flight of the ball (as it was at address) and travelling along that intended line of flight at impact with the ball and slightly beyond.

A good grip will, barring other complications in the swing, ensure both requirements are met. A bad grip will make it almost impossible to get them both right.

Angle of the Shaft

With the club correctly positioned square to the ball in front of you, apply your open left hand to the shaft. Make sure that the angle of the shaft is correctly positioned across the base of your fingers. This is critical. It should run from the middle knuckle of your forefinger to a point just below the base of your little finger.

Spacing of the Fingers

Close your hand on the shaft. Note that your last three fingers should be close together. Your forefinger should make a slight gap from the next finger to help support your thumb.

Your thumb should oppose your forefinger and be slightly off-centre, on the right of the shaft. Your thumb should never be on top of the shaft.

Firmness Test

Once you have completed the left-hand grip, try raising the head of the club with your left thumb off the shaft. If your grip is correct, your fingers will be holding the shaft secure against the fleshy pad at the heel of your hand.

HEEL PAD

The Left Hand – General Principles

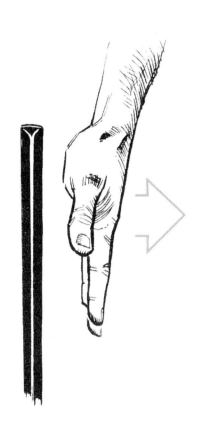

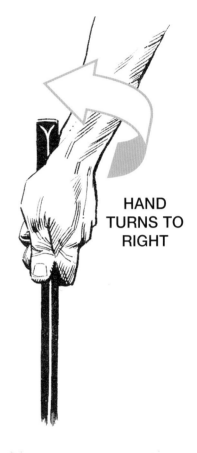

HAND TURNS TO RIGHT

1. With the club correctly positioned in front of you, align your open left palm to the shaft so that the back of your left hand squarely faces the target.

2. Close your left hand on the shaft. Your thumb will be on top of the shaft at this stage, vertically aligned with the centre of the shaft.

3. Now turn your entire left hand slightly to the right, as seen from your viewpoint, so that your left thumb moves to the right side of the shaft just a little. You have turned your left hand in this way simply to establish muscular contact between the fingers and wrist of your hand and your left forearm.

The grip
Part 2 – Right Hand

To understand where to place your right hand in the grip, think about where you would put your right hand if you were going to strike something with the palm of that hand. You would strike the object with your palm vertical and your thumb uppermost, as illustrated in fig. 2.

You would not place your hand in the position shown in the drawing below (fig. 1). The blow would lack power and you would probably hurt your hand in the process. 90 per cent of beginners and high handicap players approach the club with the right hand in this position.

Your right hand should be placed on the shaft so that the palm squarely faces the target. This is the only thing you need to think about when you are first putting your right hand in the grip.

By placing your right hand in the grip with the palm facing the target, you should immediately establish the idea that the right palm and the face of the club are aligned at all times. This is a useful concept to bear in mind, as the position of your right hand anywhere in the swing sequence should be reflected by the angle and position of the blade.

Don't do this

Fig. 1

Do this

Fig. 2

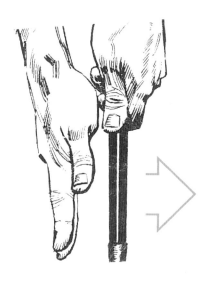

For the correct grip, your right palm squarely faces the target.

66

Your right palm and the blade should be aligned.
Both squarely face the target.

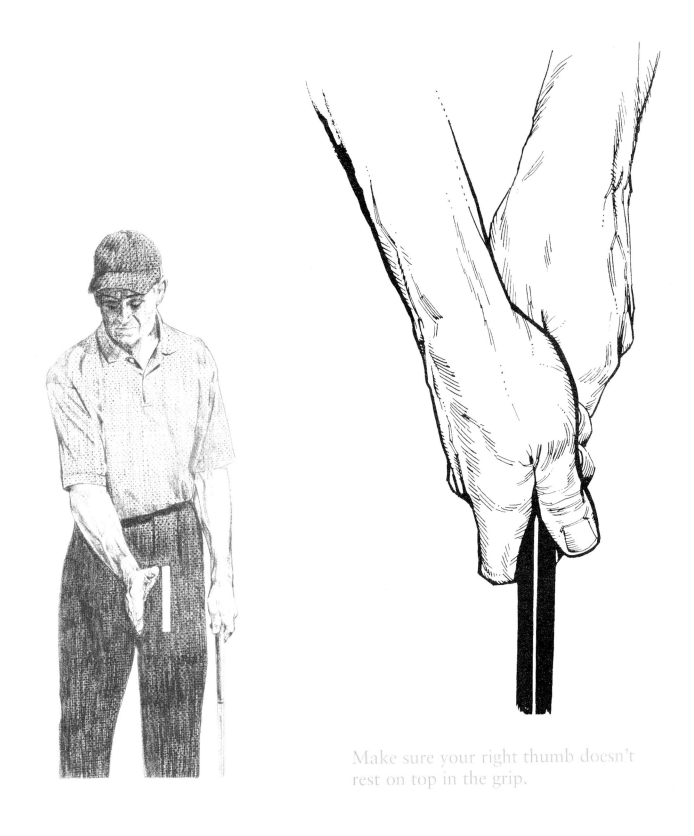

Make sure your right thumb doesn't
rest on top in the grip.

Unifying the hands to complete the grip

Now try adding the right hand to the left. Place the open palm of your right hand alongside the shaft. The palm should now be aligned with the face of the club so that they are both looking directly at the target. Don't let your hand slip from this position on the club. Close your middle fingers around the shaft, with the upper of these two fingers drawn closely against the forefinger of your left hand. Now lock your right little finger over your left forefinger, so that it rests in the space between the first two fingers of your left hand. This placement of your fingers establishes a close unity of the two hands, and is known as the Vardon overlapping grip. It has been employed by most of the world's great players, and has stood

the test of time. If you find this uncomfortable, let the hands snuggle next to each other without overlapping the fingers. This is known as the ten-finger or baseball grip.

Now to your right thumb and forefinger: your bent right forefinger should fit snugly under the shaft, slightly separated from your other fingers. The placing of your right thumb is vital. It should never be pressed on the top of the shaft. It should lie diagonally across the shaft with its tip close to or touching the tip of your right forefinger.

The control of the grip, especially of your right hand, should be felt mainly in your fingers.

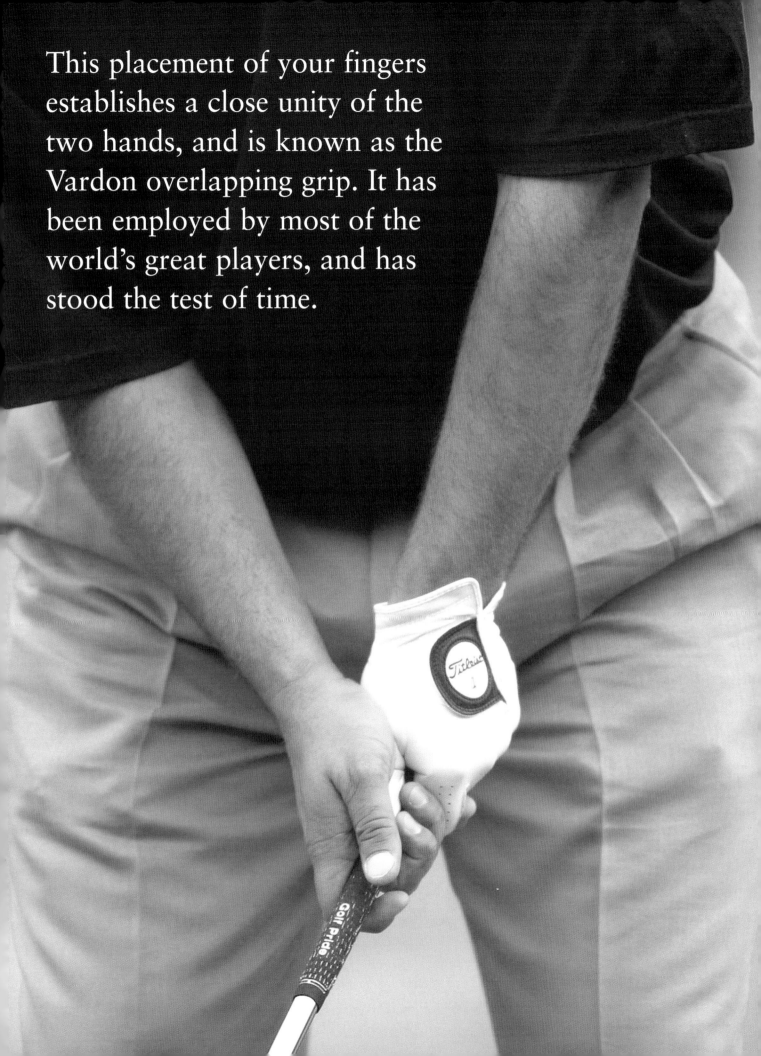

This placement of your fingers establishes a close unity of the two hands, and is known as the Vardon overlapping grip. It has been employed by most of the world's great players, and has stood the test of time.

Pressure points of the grip
Get your grip right and keep it that way

The pressure points of your grip should be through the last three fingers of your left hand, and the two middle fingers of your right hand. In other words, there should be absolutely no pressure felt between your thumbs and index fingers of either hand. If there is, your wrists and forearms are likely to stiffen and inhibit your swing.

Remember, you grip the club to swing it. You cannot swing anything effectively with too fierce a grip. Golf is not a game of force, so don't grip the club as if it were an axe. A sensitive yet firm grip is what is required: nothing more, nothing less.

Get used to the feel of the correct grip and stick to it, no matter what. If your grip is correct, and your shots are still going off line, you must look to your swing to find out what is going wrong. You simply cannot cure a bad swing by making remedial alterations to a correct grip. If you do, you are simply compounding the error. Get your grip right, and then leave it alone.

The address position

Posture

To find the correct square stance, your shoulders, hips and feet should be parallel with the intended line of flight of the ball. Your right foot may be withdrawn slightly when using a driver.

When you are standing in the address position, you are arranging your body so that you can swing the club-head along the intended line of flight of the ball. You are, in effect, adjusting the aim of the swing.

Having decided where you want the ball to go, and selected the club with the required loft to take it there, you must now establish the intended line of flight of the ball. In order to direct the swing along the intended line of flight of the ball, you must place your toes level on a second imaginary line that is parallel with the intended line of flight. Your shoulders must also be parallel with the intended line of flight.

This parallel arrangement of the toes and shoulders to the intended line of flight of the ball is known as the 'square stance'.

Keep your back relatively straight and lean over from the hips, bending the knees slightly.

Weight

Your weight should be evenly distributed between the feet, favouring neither your right nor left foot. Your weight should be supported by the whole of the underside of your feet. You mustn't throw your weight forward on to the balls of your feet, or backwards on to your heels. Your feet must feel active throughout the entire swing.

Flexed Knees

Your knees should be flexed. This is vitally important. Think of yourself as a tennis player waiting on the baseline to receive a serve. You should be alert and active, with your body poised and relaxed, ready for action. Your legs are live and fluid, like a boxer's. Your legs should be flexed and mobile. There is no room in the golf set-up for a stiff-legged stance. Stiff legs are inactive legs.

The flexing of your right leg is especially important. It is flexed in the set-up, and it will remain flexed throughout the entire backswing. There should be absolutely no straightening of your right leg during the backswing. You should make it one of your swing thoughts that the flexed position of your right leg will remain unchanged throughout your backswing.

Ball placement
Avoiding Extremes

Once you have established the intended line
of flight of the ball to the target, you should be
placing your toes level on a second imaginary line
that is parallel with the intended line of flight.

But where should the ball be in relation to your
feet in the stance?

As you move down through the bag, from
fairway woods, long irons, medium irons to the
short irons, the ball moves progressively to the
right of your stance from your viewpoint until
it reaches the halfway point between the feet.

The ball moves from the inside of your left heel
back to the halfway point, but never further back
than halfway, as you go through the bag from
long to short clubs.

BALL PLACEMENT

short irons

fairway woods and long
irons

driver

The address procedure

Stand behind the ball, looking in the direction of the shot you wish to play, and establish an imaginary line to the target. Pick out a distinct landmark or object (bush, tree, post, church spire, etc.) directly beyond the target area to serve as a specific aiming point.

You should have already chosen the club to give you the required distance for the shot you intend to play and you should now have a specific object at which to aim. Once your direction and distance have been resolved, you can concentrate solely on the shot.

While this process of evaluating the shot has been going on, you should be subconsciously forming your grip on the club, and 'feeling' the stroke in your hands. Check that the club-face is squared to your grip, then approach the ball and ground the club behind it.

When you ground the club, make sure that the face of the club is square (at right angles) to the intended line of flight of the ball.

Then position your feet by checking the aiming point that you have already chosen. Once you have placed your feet, you should be ready to play your shot.

Notice that the positioning of your feet came last.

The average golfer often reverses this procedure, placing his feet first, then, while vaguely grounding the club, he juggles with his grip in an attempt to get his club-face square.

There is no logical sequence in this method, and these last-minute grip adjustments usually account for the fact that this golfer's grip is never the same from one shot to the next.

Golf is a game of consistency. So be consistent, and develop correct routines for everything. Good golf is largely a matter of forming good habits. Here, once again, is the routine.

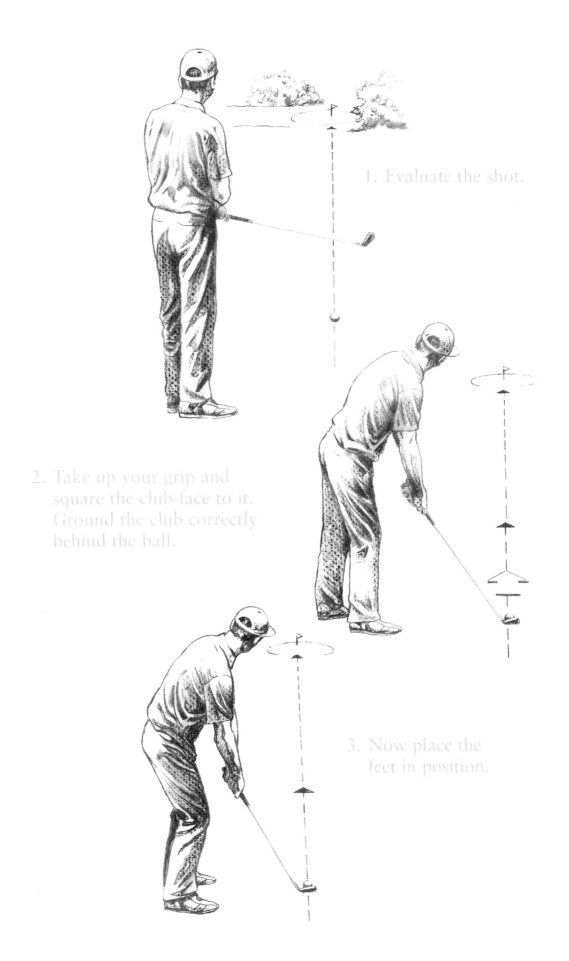

1. Evaluate the shot.

2. Take up your grip and square the club-face to it. Ground the club correctly behind the ball.

3. Now place the feet in position.

Golf is a game of consistency. So be consistent, and develop correct routines for everything. Good golf is largely a matter of forming good habits.

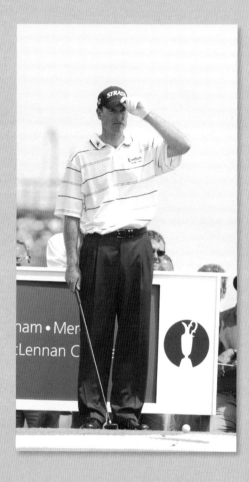

The beauty of having a swing model is that anyone can learn it – regardless of age or ability.

8 year old

Investor

Financier

Taxi driver

Address positions will vary slightly because of differences in height, body structure and the club that is used. The basic body shape, however, is the same. The back is relatively straight. The body leans forward from the hips. The knees are slightly flexed and the hands and arms are free from the body and free of tension.

'The fun you get from golf is in direct relation to the effort you don't put into it' BOB ALLEN

stage 1

The backswing
It has absolutely nothing to do with 'generating power'.

This chapter breaks the backswing down into two easy stages with exercises to help you learn. You begin with the first part of the backswing, called the takeaway, then take the club into a position halfway back, and then finally through to the top of the swing, with checkpoints to help you along the way.

Before we start it is important to understand what the backswing is for. You have probably been told that the purpose of the backswing is to generate power. Forget it. It does nothing of the kind.

Remember the five swing principles. The backswing is a precision movement that places the club-head in exactly the correct position to start the downswing. Nothing more, nothing less. It is not a dramatic wind-up of power leading to a downswing of brutal force. You do not hit the ball on the backswing; that comes later. It is simply about two things: first, correctly positioning the club at the top of the swing and, second, aligning it accurately for the downward swing into and along the intended line of flight of the ball. If the club is out of position at the top, a correct downswing will be virtually impossible without some compensatory movement.

The backswing is a precision movement and, like all other precision movements, you should perform it at moderate speed and with an absence of force. It is vital that you see your backswing as a passive phase of the swing movement. If you associate it with power and force, you will never get the club into position at the top, and the swing will be ruined.

Forget everything that you have read about the 'coiled up power of the backswing' and the 'resistance between the hips and shoulders in the backswing that is unleashed into the ball in the downswing'. These concepts stem from the myth that the backswing is for generating power.

Think of a marksman taking aim on his target. He does it calmly and with precision. The rifle must be correctly aligned before he pulls the trigger. It is similar for an archer. He positions his bow with precision before releasing the arrow. That is all you are doing in the backswing: aligning the club correctly in preparation for the 'release'. If you haven't correctly aligned or aimed it like the marksman or the archer, you are sure to be off target. It is as simple as that.

The backswing is a precision movement and, like all other precision movements, you should perform it at moderate speed and with an absence of force.

Position 1
The Takeaway

Now that you know how to address the ball, it is time to start swinging. This is the first stage of the golf swing: the takeaway. In the illustration below, the takeaway is viewed from behind the golfer, in the video position. As your hands take the club away from the ball, keep the club-face square in relation to the body. Try to remain relaxed and don't grip the club too tightly. Remember to keep your knees flexed.

As your hands begin to take the club back, your shoulders will automatically begin to turn. Your head may move almost imperceptibly to the right. The rest of your body should remain still.

1. Keep the wrist in. Notice the concave angle of the left wrist; this must stay constant throughout the backswing.

2. The club-face remains facing the ball during the first 15 cm (6 in) of the takeaway.

3. Your head will move very slightly to the right to accommodate the shoulder turn.

4. The face of the club is square in relation to the body.

5. A smooth takeaway is essential. The hands initiate the takeaway and have total control of the club throughout the swing.

Position 2
Quarter Backswing

As you take the club further back in the swing, the club-face should still remain square in relation to your body. This is crucial. If you start to change the angle, you are going wrong. Practise this until you can get it right. Most golfers are already moving off the swing plane at this point.

From where you are standing, the end of the shaft of your club should now be pointing at your left thigh and the club-head should be halfway on a line between your feet and the ball. If the club-head isn't square, check that your left wrist is 'in'.

Your shoulders should now have turned about 45 degrees in response to these movements of your hands and arms. Make sure that your left shoulder hasn't dipped in any way as it turned and that you keep your weight firmly pressed down throughout.

1. Remember that your body stays down as your arms move up.

2. The club-head is now on a line midway between the feet and the ball. The right side of your body now begins to turn over a flexed right knee as you continue to take the club back. Make sure you keep the left wrist 'in', so that you keep the face of the club square. Most golfers have by now started to roll or twist their wrists and hands.

4. Your shoulders should be turned 45 degrees.

3. Your left shoulder should maintain a constant height.

5. Your hands and the end of the shaft of the club should be pointing towards the left thigh.

6. The face of the club should remain square in relation to your body.

Position 3
Halfway Back

Now you are going to take your club halfway back. If you can complete this move consistently, you are on the way to a very good swing.

Remember to keep your weight down and your head still. By now your hands should be in line with your left hip. Keep your knees flexed; don't let the right knee begin to straighten or your weight begin to rise. Notice how if you were looking at a line continuing along the shaft of the club, it would be pointing midway between the ball and the feet.

1. A good general rule is to have the shaft pointing down the middle of the right forearm.

2. If the line of the shaft continued, it would be pointing midway between the ball and the feet.

3. Your body stays down
as your arm moves up.
Your head remains still.

4. Your hands and left arm
are opposite or 'in line'
with the left hip.

5. Your knees have
remained flexed.

6. The angle of the shaft will vary
slightly with different clubs.

The wrists must not roll during the takeaway

The key mistake that the vast majority of players make is that of rolling their wrists 'open' or 'closed' during the takeaway, altering the alignment of the face of the club to the ball. Remember that the club-face was square at the address, and it must remain square throughout your swing. So, when the club-face returns to the ball at impact, it should still be square, or at right angles to the intended line of flight. During the takeaway, therefore, the club-face must be at right angles to the swing path at all times.

If you stick to this simple rule, you won't make the mistake of rolling your wrists.

During the takeaway,
therefore, the club-face
must be at right angles to
the swing path at all times.

Halfway back, club-face check

At the halfway stage of the backswing, the club-face should be vertical (as illustrated) if you haven't rolled your wrists.

If the club-face is open at this stage, you have rolled your wrists in a clockwise direction. If the club is in the 'shut' position, that is,

'looking at the ground', you have rolled your wrists in an anticlockwise direction.

If you can keep your club-face at the correct, 'square' position at the halfway stage, the hands and arm will swing to the top, placing the face at the correct angle at the top of the swing.

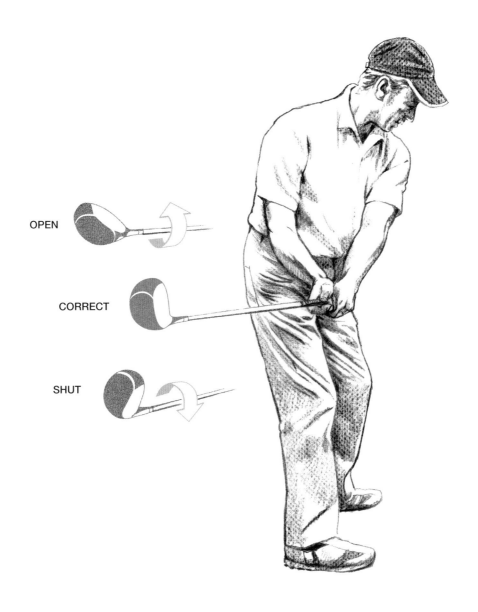

OPEN

CORRECT

SHUT

Good and bad – a comparison

Good

By now you should be able to take
the club back in one piece. A line
drawn through the shaft and your
hands would point between your
feet and the ball.

Bad

Make sure that you are not twisting
or rolling the club-head away from the
ball in the first metre (few feet) of the
swing. At halfway back, a line drawn
through the shaft and hands would be
almost parallel to the ground.

How to do it

These pictures show Swing Factory regulars lining up with Nick Faldo and Ernie Els to demonstrate the halfway back position. Although the clubs in their hands may be different, the basic position is the same. The knees are flexed, the shoulders and hips have begun to turn and, above all, the shaft runs roughly down the right forearm. A line drawn as a continuation of the shaft would point somewhere between the feet and the ball.

If you can do this consistently, you've mastered one of the trickiest parts of the swing and are almost ready to complete the backswing. At a later stage, when you are out on the course, if you find yourself losing your swing, go back to the takeaway. Chances are that this is where things are going wrong. Don't let anyone tell you otherwise.

One of the Swing Factory's most famous pupils regularly plays with some of the best golfers in the world and has access to all the help he ever needs from them and their coaches. Unfortunately, when things go wrong, he gets confused by so much conflicting advice and he usually ends up in more of a mess than ever. Whenever he returns to the school, it is invariably in the takeaway that he has slipped up.

If you can do this consistently, you've mastered one of the trickiest parts of the swing and are almost ready to complete the backswing.

Britain's most successful

Thespian

PR consultant

Goalkeeper

World number two

TV presenter

Coach

Model

Lawyer

Exercise A
Arms in front

Here are three exercises to help you reinforce the halfway back position. The halfway back position is not only essential in building the full swing, it forms the foundation of the short game when combined with the half finish, which you will learn in stage 4. Later on you will find hitting shots from halfway back to halfway through will give you a real sense of timing and tempo.

1. Hold the club directly in front of you.

2. Now turn your feet and body 90 degrees to the left.

3. Put your head down as if you were looking at the ball.

You should now be in the perfect position. This exercise will give you a useful check to see if you are getting into the correct halfway back position.

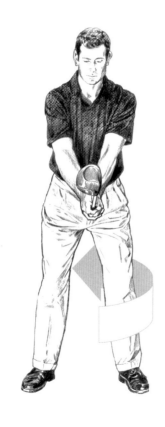

Exercise B

Split hands

1. Split the hands, gripping the right hand 15–18 cm (6–7 in) below the left hand.

2. Take your address.

3. Now take the club back to halfway.

More than any other, this exercise gives you the feeling of a correct takeaway.

Exercise C
Leslie King's signature exercise

This exercise was first used by Leslie King in the 1930s. It is now employed by a number of excellent teachers and so it should be. It creates the perfect halfway back position.

1. Assume the address position.

2. Keeping the body down, lift the arms in front of you to waist height.

3. Turn your shoulders to the right, taking care not to twist the wrists or move your head.

Address

Practice swing

Ball swing

Left-hander Mike Weir knows the importance of a good takeaway. The next time you see him on TV, notice how he takes the club back to halfway twice before taking his full swing. Weir feels that he has to exaggerate his practice swing in order to keep the club on line. This is a very good way of keeping your swing shape. You should think in terms of exaggerating the correct hand movement on the takeaway to ensure you get it right.

How not to do it

As this is one of the most important parts of the method, it is worth having yet another look at it. Here are some Swing Factory visitors showing us how they start their backswing on their first visit. Look carefully and you should be able to see what they are doing wrong in the takeaway. They are, of course, making the same disastrous error – rolling their wrists. Make sure that you don't join them. Most golfers are in the same bad position halfway through their backswing. This is the curse of golf, and even the greatest player in the world is prone to it. Do this and you are in the golfing equivalent of intensive care with your chances of recovery being slim.

In the illustration below, the player has twisted or rolled the club-head away from the ball in the first metre (few feet) of the backswing as he is going halfway back. A line drawn through the shaft and hands would be almost parallel to the ground. And by twisting or rolling the club-head on the takeaway, he has destroyed his chances of a good swing.

It is hard to get it right consistently. Even scratch players and touring professionals are constantly struggling to maintain a consistent takeaway. The greatest player in the world admits that he is prone to it. When Tiger Woods starts to struggle with his driving, you can be sure it is because his hands and club-head have begun to twist around his body.

The golf swing is a series of chain reactions, and one good position allows you to go to the next. Conversely, one bad position will invariably lead to another. By mastering each one, you are giving yourself a great chance of long-term improvement. If you go wrong at this early stage in the swing, you are in trouble. Check on your video that you have got this stage right before you move on.

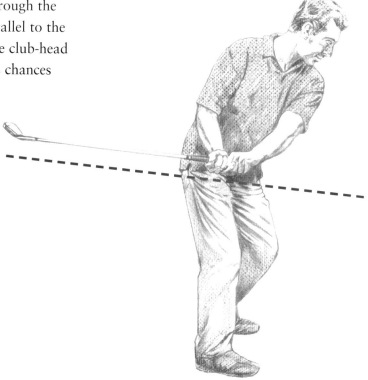

Gigolo   Radiographer   Film star

Legend   Headmaster   Actor

Publisher   Sportsman   Financier

'The golf swing is like sex. You can't be thinking about the mechanics of the act while you are performing'
DAVE HILL

stage 2

Position 4
Top of the Backswing

At the top of your backswing, the inside of your left arm should be opposite your right shoulder. Your left wrist should remain slightly cupped. Your head should have moved very slightly to allow your shoulders to make their complete turn. Remember that your left shoulder should remain at the same height to the ground throughout the swing.

1. With an iron, the shaft appears slightly 'laid off'; with a wood, the shaft would be horizontal to the ground and parallel to the line of flight.

2. The inside of your left arm should be opposite your right shoulder.

3. Your left wrist should be
   slightly 'cupped'.

4. The head has moved
   slightly to the right
   to allow a full
   shoulder turn.

5. The weight remains down through
   the legs and feet, and the body has
   maintained a constant height
   throughout the backswing.

The angle of the club-face at the top is critical

If your grip is correct, and if you haven't rolled your wrists or introduced other errors in the takeaway and backswing, you will be able to find the correct blade angle at the top of your swing. Then, when you bring the club-face back to the ball in the downswing, it will be square, just as it was at the address.

If you have rolled your wrists during the takeaway and backswing, the blade angle at the top is bound to be incorrect; it will be either 'open' or 'shut'. Then you will have to use a corresponding amount of wrist-roll in the opposite direction during the downswing in order to square up the blade at impact. This precise and delicate operation is impossible to do consistently. And what is more, it is an unnecessary complication that can be avoided.

If your swing is sound, you will automatically get the correct blade angle at the top of your backswing, ensuring a solid, square impact with the ball in your downswing.

Open

Here the angle between the back of the left hand and the forearm is much too pronounced. The wrist is far too 'cupped' and the club-face is consequently 'open'. This is called a 'concave position' of the left wrist.

Shut

Here is the opposite extreme. Because the hand is dropped below the line of the forearm, the left wrist is in a convex position 'shutting' the blade. This hand position is comparatively rare among high handicappers, and tends to promote a smother or a hook. A hook is the constant enemy of all 'shut-faced' players. Don't flirt with this method. You may well see some of the top players in this position at the top. Don't copy them. These 'shut-faced' players combine this wrist position with a special type of body action in the downswing which enables them to return the club-face to square at impact.

Correct

Here again is the correct left wrist position at the top and the correct blade angle that goes with it: a slightly 'cupped' wrist and a blade angle at about 30 degrees off the vertical. A correct grip, a square face at address, absence of wrist-roll in the backswing, and a correct body turn combine to create this position.

So, remember, the correct blade angle at the top coupled with a correct downswing movement will automatically produce a dead square impact of club with ball, which is the secret of long, accurate shot-making.

Open

Shut

Correct

The slightly 'cupped' left wrist is the key to the correct blade angle at the top

This is how your hands should look at the top of the backswing. The angle of the club-face (or blade) at the top is governed by the angle that the back of your left hand makes with your left forearm. At the top of the swing your left wrist should be slightly 'cupped'. In the illustration below, the angle formed between the back of the left hand and the forearm should be about 30 degrees. This is ideal. This wrist position will place the club-face at a correct angle, with the leading edge of the club vertical or inclined at an angle of about 30 degrees to the vertical or somewhere between these two. All other angles at the top are incorrect and will lead to inaccuracy and loss of power. Check on the video or in the mirror that this is what your hand, wrist and club-face look like.

Square   30° closed

Both these blade angles are acceptable

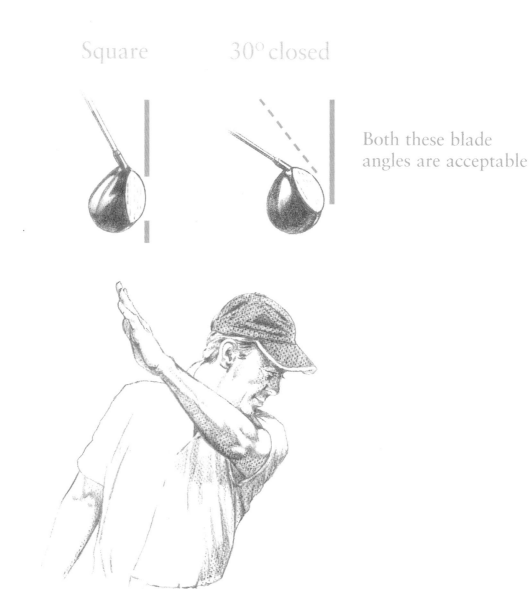

The 'laid-off' shaft

Don't get confused when you pick up a wood. Below are two illustrations of the completed backswing with a medium iron and a driver. See how the shaft of the driver is horizontal to the ground and parallel with the intended line of flight of the ball. The shaft of the iron, however, has stopped well short of the horizontal and so appears to be 'laid off', as we say. This is entirely correct.

Although the two swings appear different, they are not. The shaft of the driver reaches a near horizontal position simply because of the additional wrist action that naturally occurs with the longer clubs. The shorter distance shots are naturally more firm-wristed. That alone accounts for the different positions of the shafts.

It is important to realise that if the medium iron swing were to be completed, its shaft would reach exactly the same position as the shaft of the driver and the blade angles of both clubs would be identical.

Both clubs are on line but one has simply gone back further than the other. So, from the view from behind the golfer, the laid-off shaft when you use your irons is entirely correct.

One final point. Many golfers are under the impression that the swings with irons and woods are different.

The basic swing action with all clubs is the same. The amount of turn with all clubs is the same. The only difference in the final position of the shafts is accounted for at the top of the swing by the additional natural wrist action employed with the driver and longer clubs.

Why a full shoulder turn is necessary

Many of the world's top golfers say that a full shoulder turn is necessary for power. But you will remember that the backswing has nothing to do with generating power. Its purpose is simply to position the club correctly at the top in readiness for the downward swing. It is a mistake to associate the backswing with power. After all, you don't hit the ball on the backswing. Hitting the ball comes later. Thinking 'power' tends to make the backswing quick and jerky, and this results in an incomplete turn.

Your backswing thought should not be about 'a full shoulder turn in order to generate power'. Instead, you should remember that a full shoulder turn allows the hands and arms to swing fully into a correct position at the top. From there they can swing down into the ball on a correct line through impact. This is what creates power and straightness.

Complete the backswing first. Do it smoothly and with plenty of time. Power is released at a late stage in the downswing. Don't run ahead of the correct sequence.

A full turn is vital to position the club correctly at the top

It is not enough just to turn your shoulders, the right side of your body from your hip to your shoulder must also move to get a full turn. But as your right hip goes back, you must not let it rise up. If it does, your right leg is straightening. Your right leg must stay flexed throughout your backswing.

Similarly, your left shoulder must not drop during the turn. It simply moves across, maintaining a constant height from the ground. This is vital.

As your arms swing the club up, your body stays down

As your hands and arms swing the club back and up, there should be a distinct feeling, particularly in the knees and feet, that the body is staying down. You should feel a downward pressure through the feet.

By pressing your feet into the ground, it will increase the leverage developed by your hands and arms as they swing upward.

If you allow your body to rise up as your hands and arms swing up, you immediately destroy the capacity of your hands and arms to swing.

Remember that any hint of upward lift or sway in the body during the backswing literally takes the power out of your hands and arms and your swing.

The role of the legs and feet in the backswing
The Flexed Right Leg

Why is the flexed right leg so important? Because you need it flexed so that you turn your body correctly. By keeping your right leg flexed, your head is held at a constant height from the ground, stopping it from bobbing up and down.

As you turn towards the top of the backswing, your right hip moves back, but it mustn't rise up. If you straighten your right leg during the backswing, a full hip and shoulder turn will be virtually impossible. And what is more, your head will tip over in the direction of the target. Then the shape of the body turn will be destroyed, as will the plane of the backswing. If this happens, the club is bound to be out of position at the top of the backswing.

Your flexed right leg will steady the body as it turns. Then, by turning correctly, your body will make a full, free swing of your hands and arms possible. If your club is being moved by your body swaying or heaving, then the line of your arm swing is destroyed. So a correctly shaped body movement will help to create a full and free swing of your hands and arms.

That is why keeping your right leg flexed during the backswing is vital. It promotes the type of turn that allows your hands and arms to swing properly. If you straighten the right leg, it will destroy your turn and, with it, your swing.

The position of the right leg remains unchanged throughout the backswing

Once you have correctly placed your right leg at the address, its position should remain virtually unchanged throughout the backswing. As you now know, you turn your body over the flexed right leg. This supports the swing and stops you from swaying so a real turn can take place.

There shouldn't be a marked weight shift from your left foot to your right foot during the backswing. At the completion of your backswing, your weight should still be more or less evenly distributed between your feet, as it was at the address.

Throughout your backswing, your weight should be concentrated on the insides of the balls of your feet. You should notice a slight knock-kneed feeling at all times, just as there should be at the address.

To get a proper sense of the supporting role of your flexed right leg in your backswing, try placing a golf ball under the outside of your right foot. This transfers the weight to the inside of your foot where it should be, and the vital stabilising task of your right leg during the backswing becomes clear. Feel how much firmer it makes the backswing movement.

The backswing problem
Turning Your Body Correctly

One of the main principles of the Swing Factory is that the hands, arms and body must move in unison throughout the swing. They move simultaneously, as if they are shadowing each other. But they do have very different roles. The body turns and moves simply to make way for an unrestricted swing of the hands and arms.

One of the most common mistakes in the backswing is to move your body in a way that blocks or restricts your hands and arms from making a good swing.

Throughout your backswing, your body and hips must turn while maintaining a constant height, and you do this by keeping your right knee flexed. This is where most golfers go wrong. They tend to straighten their right knee as they swing the club back, lifting their right hip and shoulder. This blocks the free swing of their hands and arms and distorts the club-line.

Bad

This is where most golfers go wrong. They tend to straighten their right knee as they swing the club back, lifting their right hip and shoulder. This blocks the free swing of their hands and arms and distorts the club-line.

Bad

A sure test of correct body shape

Notice the shape of the good player's body. The line down his back to his hip forms a convex curve. The body curves slightly away from the target. This convex body shape when the club is at the top of the backswing is common to all good golfers and is, in fact, the result of a correct series of movements in the backswing.

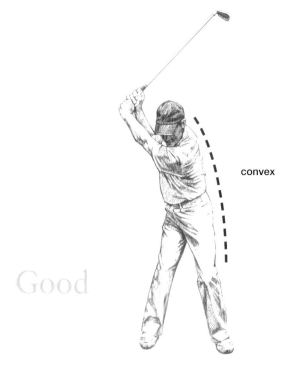

convex

Good

Contrast it with the concave body shape below (right). Here the player's body curves towards the target. This posture is the result of the incorrect body movement in the backswing.

Check your body shape in a mirror. If it is slightly convex, you can be sure your turn is substantially correct. If it is concave, you should go back to stage 1 and start again.

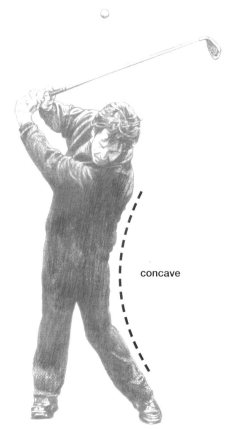

concave

Bad

Top of your backswing – a reminder of the crucial points

By now you should have learned how to complete your backswing. You have learned it in stages because each phase, if carried out correctly, creates the conditions for carrying out the next and subsequent phases. In the same way, any error at any stage will be carried over into the next stage.

To begin with, your swing will feel like a series of separate movements. Now you must work on feeling the backswing as one fluid, strain-free action. You have to learn to let your hands and arms swing properly. Remember that your body turns so the hands and arms can swing freely.

You should also understand all the mechanics required to ensure your backswing's success. This will help you in the challenge to perfect the correct movement until it is automatic and engrained in your subconscious.

Above all, remember you are not trying to hit the ball on the backswing. You are merely positioning yourself for the downward swing of the club. Smoothness, ease of effort, and control are the watchwords here. If you think about hitting, the tension in your hands and arms will destroy the free swing.

Just focus on training your body to move in unison with the swing of your arms. Forget the ball. Control the impulse to hit and your backswing will become the foundation of a sound, controlled swing.

Once again, make sure you have got the backswing rules firmly in mind.

First and most important, the backswing is performed solely to place the club in the correct position at the top. To get the club in the right position at the top, your shoulders are fully turned through 90 degrees, your left shoulder has not dropped as it came round to meet your chin, the right side of the body from your hip to your shoulder has been fully cleared

to the rear, your hips have turned through 45 degrees, your right leg is still flexed and your left heel has stayed down.

Remember that the shaft of the club must be parallel with the intended line of flight of the ball or 'laid off' behind your hands. The shaft must on no account point across the intended line of flight, that is, to the right of the target. If you find yourself in this across-line position at the top, it will lead to endless complications in the downswing and is, in fact, the result of an incorrect backswing. Check that you have really got this right before you move on to the next chapter.

Without a controlled backswing you are nowhere.

The beauty of having a swing model is that anyone can learn, regardless of age or ability.

Just to reassure you that anyone of any age or ability can find the correct positions for playing great golf, here is a backswing gallery featuring an octogenarian, a furniture-maker, a fisherman and a model, and some leading professionals that you might recognise, at the top of their backswings.

Although their positions vary very slightly, this is due to their differing physical characteristics or their choice of club. The basic swing shape is the same. The shoulders have turned 90 degrees, the hips have turned and the flexed right knee has supported the turn of the backswing. The weight has stayed down as the hands and arms have swung up. The length of the swing is contained and the blade angle is square or at an angle of 30 degrees.

Check on your video or in the mirror that you can consistently reach this position. If you can, then it is time to move on.

'Our doubts are traitors, and make us lose the good we oft might win, by fearing to attempt'

WILLIAM SHAKESPEARE

stage 3

Starting Down
The transition from the backswing to the downswing – the slowest phase of the swing

Now that you have understood in some detail exactly what you should feel at the top of the swing, you can move on to think about exactly how your downswing should be carried out. You know that the backswing has nothing to do with generating power; it should be smooth, unhurried and strain-free. You are merely positioning the hands, club and body correctly before starting the downward swing. If you have got this right at the top of your backswing and therefore at the beginning of your downswing, your hands will automatically acquire potential power at the top.

At the top, the swing slows down. In fact, the transition from backswing to downswing is the slowest part of the swing. This accentuates and amplifies the feeling of conserved power in your hands. Now you should begin to anticipate what we call the release, the moment that you bring real power into the swing. But at this stage you should only anticipate it. You need to conserve that power until you are halfway down. Only then does the release kick in. If you can understand that this feeling of power at the top depends on you having a passive, controlled backswing in the first place, then you are on the way. But if you have made the hacker's mistake of applying force in the backswing and putting power into your hands too early, you will have jumped the gun and charged your hands too soon.

This will make you release power too soon in the downswing, and nothing on earth can stop it. In other words, by applying force in your backswing, you lose your timing, hit from the top of the swing, throw your shoulders into it and destroy the whole movement. This impatience to 'hit' is extremely common. It happens when you don't trust your swing and is a result of thinking about the backswing in terms of generating power.

Direction and power

The purpose of the downswing is to achieve a powerful, square impact into and along the intended line of flight of the ball.

Remember the swing plane diagram and the line the club must take. You want to hit the ball straight and long, so the club must swing down from the top on an arc that will cause it automatically to swing into and along the intended line of flight of the ball through impact and beyond. This is the principle upon which a successful downswing is based.

In a correct downswing, the hands, shaft and club-head must remain on that swing plane at all times. Only then can the club-head end up swinging along the intended line of flight.

Developing power in the swing depends to a very large extent on swinging the club on a correct downswing line. Power and direction are closely related. An incorrect downswing line tends to destroy power. And obviously, there is no point in developing power if it is not combined with direction. If you do this, you are simply knocking the ball further into trouble.

The purpose of the downswing is to achieve
a powerful, square impact into and along
the intended line of flight of the ball.

Position 5
Halfway Down

Now you are going to start your downswing. This is how you should look halfway down. Notice how the club-face has remained square in relation to your body. If you look at yourself in the mirror position, the club-head should be facing it and you.

From your perspective, the club-head should be on the swing plane slightly behind your right shoulder. Your hips should have returned to almost the same position they were in at the address.

Your head should have remained centred and your shoulders should still be almost fully turned. Look carefully at the position of the wrists. See how they have stayed hinged as they enter what is called the 'area of release'. You should feel that your hands are controlling the club through your fingers. As your hands and arms come down, your weight should move immediately towards your left foot. There should be a small lateral shift of your body as your weight becomes evenly distributed between both feet.

1. The club-head is on plane and slightly behind the right shoulder.

2. The hips have returned to almost the same position they were in at the address.

3. Your head should remain centred, and your shoulders should still be almost fully turned.

4. The club-face faces the wall or mirror in front of you.

5. The club-face should be square in relation to your body.

6. Your wrists should be hinged as they enter the release area. The hands retain control of the club through the fingers. As the hands and arms swing the club down, the weight moves towards the left foot. There is a small lateral shift as the weight is evenly distributed between the right and left feet.

Position 6
Impact

Now it is time to bring your club into the impact position. Notice how, by keeping the club-face square in relation to the body throughout the backswing and the downswing, it has returned to strike the ball in the middle of the club-face.

Your head is still centred. Your shoulders are beginning to open out towards the intended line of flight and your hips should also have turned at least 45 degrees. By now your hands should have almost returned to the same position they were in when they first addressed the ball. Notice in the diagram how the right knee has folded in towards the target. Most important of all is that from halfway down to impact is the moment of release. From the halfway down position, the right hand has released the club-head into the back of the ball. This is where the power comes into the shot. Remember not to bring the power into the swing too early. It destroys the club-line. You should not be thinking about power in the backswing or at the top of the downswing. It is only here, from halfway down to impact, that the power of the swing comes through.

The club-head should never overtake your hands or your hands be ahead of the club-head. Your hands, arms and the club should be travelling on a long, straight line – the apex of the swing plane.

1. Your club-face should be square as it hits the ball in the middle of the club-face.

144

2. Your shoulders should be square or very slightly open and your hips should be turned a minimum of 45 degrees.

3. Your head should be centred.

4. Your hands should return to almost the same position as they were in at the address.

5. Your right knee folds in towards the target.

6. From the halfway down position, your right hand has released the club-head into the back of the ball. At no time should the club-head overtake your hands nor must your hands be ahead of the club-head. The club-head should be travelling on a long, straight line.

Exercise A
The swing and stop

Here is a brilliant exercise to help you get into
the correct impact position. You should use
it in your practice sessions when you warm
up and also to help you find your swing on the
golf course. It teaches you to create a square
impact off the middle of the blade.

Remember that the hands, shaft and club-head
are vertically aligned at the moment
of impact and the face of the club is square
(at right angles) to the intended line of flight
of the ball.

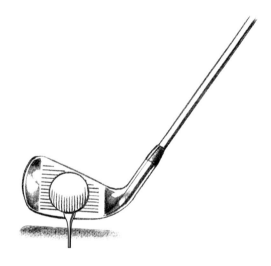

Take a 5-iron and go through your normal
swing action, but stop the club at impact.
Do not go through the finish.

Practise this exercise and see if you can find the
middle of the blade. It is not as easy as you think.

The swing and stop exercise. Swing Factory regulars line up to show you how it should be done.

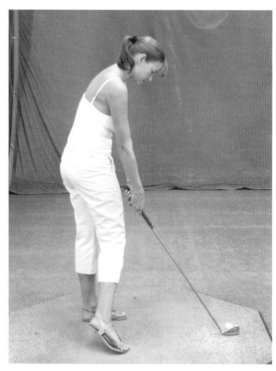

How not to do it

Father
Personal trainer
Critic

Networker
Son
Milliner

Tennis pro
8 year old
Rock icon

Here again is the rogues' gallery demonstrating how not to do it. These photos show you how most golfers look at impact when they first visit the Swing Factory. Look carefully. Can you see how static each player is? Notice how their hips haven't turned, their feet and legs are not connected to the movement of the hands and arms. This means that they have very little chance of making sustained contact with the ball.

Bad   Good

Look at the video of your swing. If your downswing sequence has returned you to this position at impact, even the best backswing in the world would make no difference to your golf whatsoever.

Every good golfer, no matter what route they have taken on the backswing, will return to the impact position with the body and legs turning through the ball, allowing the hands and arms to drive the ball forward. Make sure you can do this before you move on to the next chapter.

'All that we are is a result of what we have thought' Buddha

stage 4

Position 7
The Quarter Finish

You have completed the strike of the ball and now you begin your follow-through or finish. Notice how the club-face has continued to remain square in relation to your body. This shows you how your hands and arms should have moved in unison with your body throughout the swing.

Your arms are now extended in front of you, but you still feel a sense of them being linked to the rest of your body. Your right knee has now folded in towards the target. Your hips should have turned at least 45 degrees. Your right heel has left the ground.

1. The club-face should remain square in relation to your body.

2. Your right heel has left the ground.

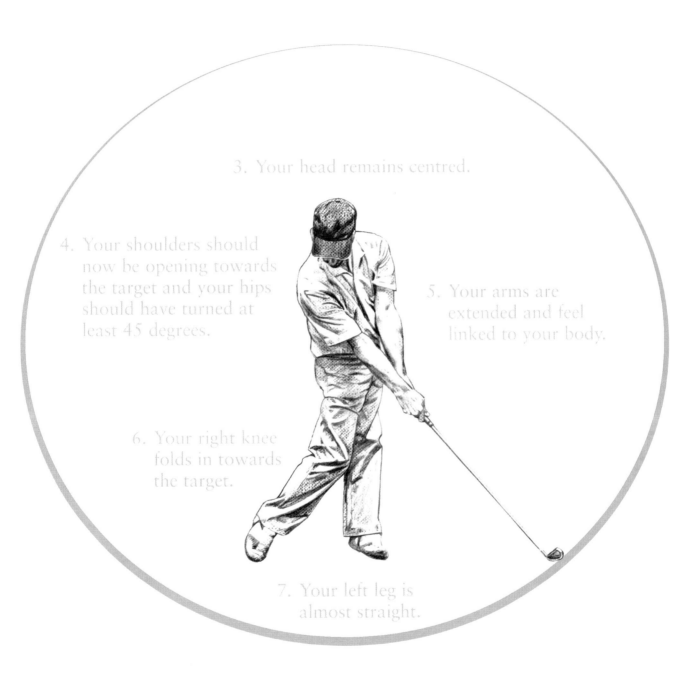

3. Your head remains centred.

4. Your shoulders should now be opening towards the target and your hips should have turned at least 45 degrees.

5. Your arms are extended and feel linked to your body.

6. Your right knee folds in towards the target.

7. Your left leg is almost straight.

Every top player, no matter what route they have taken through the swing, is in an identical position just after impact.

Exercise A
The quarter finish

The quarter finish is a crucial position for all golfers to master. Every top player, no matter what route they have taken through the swing, is in an almost identical position just after impact. The position is called the quarter finish.

Here are some exercises that will help you to understand and acquire the feeling required to commit the quarter finish to your muscle memory.

You can practise this drill anywhere. If you are doing it outside, tee up the ball. If you are indoors, use a plastic ball or even a rolled up ball of paper.

Place a club between the heel of the right foot and the big toe of the left foot, and one between the left heel and right big toe.

Take your address and make a quarter backswing. Now play the ball to the position where the shaft of the club is lying.

The face of the club should be perfectly aligned with the shaft.

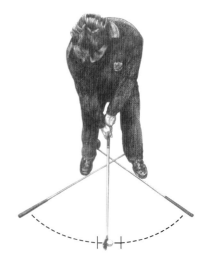

Exercise B
Split hands

Keeping the clubs between the feet, grip the
club with the right hand 13–15 cm (5–6 in)
below the left.

Place the left arm on the body with the butt
of the shaft touching the belly button.

Swing back to a quarter backswing. Now feel
that the whole right side of the body is turning
through to the quarter finish. You should feel
how the body, hands and arms have stayed
'connected' throughout the whole movement.

Once again, as in the previous exercise, the blade
of the club should be squarely aligned with the
shaft on the ground.

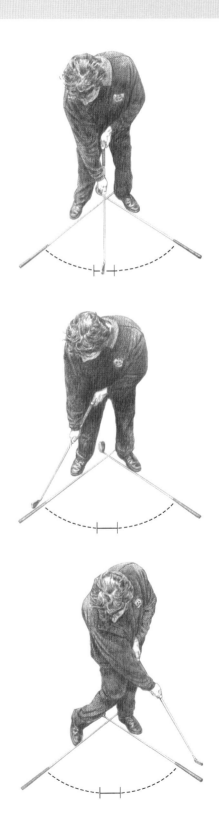

Exercise C

Swing and stop at the quarter finish

This is a very good exercise to link up everything you have learned so far. It is also a very good warm-up exercise for when you are practising or going out to play. It is an extension of the swing and stop exercise from the previous chapter. By now you should be able to hit shots using a full backswing and stopping at the quarter finish position. Obviously, the speed of the swing will be curtailed a little. (We recommend about a quarter of normal speed.) If the movement is correct, you will be surprised by how far the ball will go.

If you are using a golf ball outside, make sure you tee the ball up at the address. Then take the club back to the top of the backswing and pause slightly. Now play the ball, stopping your swing at the quarter finish position.

STOP

STOP

A quarter finish comparison

Just to give you the confidence that anyone can find the swing positions as well as the top tour professionals, here are some beginners from the Swing Factory in the quarter finish position. Each one is paired against a tour professional. It is hard to tell the difference.

Model

Greg Norman

Taxi driver

José Maria Olazabal

Swing Factory beginners verses Open Championship contenders

Financier

Charles Howell III

News presenter

Davis Love III

Every top player will return to an almost identical position at the quarter finish.

Position 8
The Half Finish

You are now halfway through your follow-through or finish. Again the club-face should have remained square to your body. It should now be at exactly 90 degrees from its original angle in the address position.

Your hips should be almost facing the target, and from your viewpoint your hands and your arms should be just inside the line of your right hip. Your left leg should be almost completely straight. Notice that your head has remained stationary and is still the same height from the ground.

1. Your club-face should be square in relation to your body.

2. Your hands and arms are just inside the line of your right hip.

3. Your hips are almost facing the target.

4. Your head has still not
   moved and is at the same
   height to the ground.

5. The left leg is
   almost straight.

Exercise A

Arms in front

1. Having taken your address position,
   keep the body down and lift the
   arms in front of you to waist height.

2. Turn your feet and body 90 degrees
   to the left, taking care not to twist
   the wrists. Bring your right foot into
   the finish position as you turn.

Notice how similar both sides of the golf swing are. Patricia, a Swing Factory beginner, here demonstrates the Leslie King halfway back drill followed by the halfway through drill.

If she had selected a lofted iron and adopted a slightly open stance (where the left foot is drawn back from the right), her halfway back, halfway through drill would teach her the basic approach shot.

Exercise B

One-handed half finish

This exercise is very important to work on as it helps you to develop the right club-line through the ball. It also gives you a great feeling for the correct moment of release of the body and club-head through the ball.

1. Tee up the ball, swing the club down to waist height. Take your left hand off the club and place it by your left side. Play the shot by releasing the right hand in unison with the turn of the right side of the body.

2. Follow through to hip height, checking that the face of the club has remained square. If the blade has turned over to the left, the ball will hook. If it is held open (like a cover drive in cricket), the ball will push to the right.

Exercise C

Hitting shots to the half finish

Once you are comfortable with your half swing exercise, you should be able to hit shots stopping at the half finish position. Once again, the speed of the swing will be slightly slower (about 50 per cent of a full swing) but you should still be able to hit the ball a surprisingly good distance. This exercise will be a real help in building a good club-line through the ball.

Notice how the basic shape
of all four professionals'
hands, arms and hips is the
same at the half finish.

The half finish

From film star to DJ: two Swing Factory pupils show how their swings match those of the masters.

Swing Factory regular Christopher Lee still plays off a handicap of 7, even though he is over eighty years old. His favourite professional golfer is Davis Love III. Here his half finish position matches that of his golfing hero.

DJ Spoony, a recent convert to the game of golf, is a deep admirer of Tiger Woods. Their half finishes, both on the course and practised indoors, are almost indistinguishable.

Position 9
The Three-quarter Finish

You are almost there. Here are two illustrations of the three-quarter finish. Yet again the club-face is still square in relation to the body. Your body should remain centred with your right knee now pointing directly to the target.

By now your shoulders should have turned a complete 90 degrees with your hands and arms in line with your left shoulder from the video position behind you. Your hips should also have turned a full 90 degrees from the address position.

Your head will have turned with your shoulders but remained centred and at the same height from the ground. Your left leg should now be completely straight.

1. Your hands and arms should be in line with your left shoulder.

2. Your shoulders have turned through 90 degrees.

3. Your hips have turned 90 degrees.

4. Your club-face should be
square in relation to the body.

5. Your body should
be centred.

6. Your right knee
points to the target.

It is an outstanding illustration of
Faldo's pure hand line and perfect body
poise through to the three-quarter finish.

This picture of Nick Faldo has been used by the Swing Factory for the last ten years. It is an outstanding illustration of Faldo's pure hand line and perfect body poise through to the three-quarter finish. The shape of the hands, the left elbow and right arm are straight out of a textbook. The blade is square. The picture was taken in Dubai in 1994 and there aren't many better examples of the perfect three-quarter finish.

If you have recorded your swing on video from this angle, your hands and arms should appear to be in line with your left shoulder.

The three-quarter finish

The three-quarter finish has been taught at the Swing Factory for over fifty years and is fast becoming a common sight on the professional tour. Its popularity can be attributed to Tiger Woods who, when faced with a particularly challenging tee-shot, will generally select a 3-iron and, using a three-quarter finish, drive the ball long and low down the centre of the fairway.

With beginners, the Swing Factory initially teaches no more than a three-quarter finish in order to build a more controlled movement through the ball. This stops you from twisting or breaking your wrists at and beyond impact with the ball. It also prevents any premature splaying of the elbows through the finish.

Its popularity can be attributed to Tiger Woods who, when faced with a particularly challenging tee-shot, will generally select a 3-iron and, using a three-quarter finish, drive the ball long and low down the centre of the fairway.

Exercise D

Three-quarter finish

Hitting shots to a three-quarter finish is a great exercise and will prove to be an invaluable weapon in your armoury. These shots should be played at 75 per cent of your normal swing speed.

1. Tee up and address the ball.

2. Pause slightly at the
   top of the backswing.

3. Play the ball holding
   the finish at the three-
   quarter position.

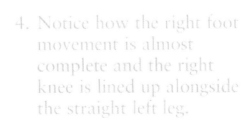

4. Notice how the right foot
   movement is almost
   complete and the right
   knee is lined up alongside
   the straight left leg.

Position 10
The Full Finish or Follow-through

This is the final position in the golf swing. Notice that your hands and arms should be completely relaxed. Your body and hips should now face the target. Your right foot is balanced on the toe. Now the swing is complete.

Practise holding this position for an extra five seconds at the end of every swing in order to familiarise yourself with the finishing position and to remind yourself always to complete your swing.

1. Your hands and arms should be completely relaxed.

2. Your body and hips face the target.

3. Your right foot should be up on its big toe.

4. Your right knee
should be pointing
towards the target.

5. Your left leg should
be straight.

If you have recorded yourself on video, your follow-through, from the camera's angle, should look something like this.

Club-face check at finish

This is a very good exercise to use to check your blade angle at the finish. Having completed the follow-through, let the hands drop back to hip level, placing the shaft of the club at an angle of about 45 degrees to the ground and parallel with the intended line of flight. Now check that the face of the club is still square. The leading edge of the club-face or blade should be vertical when you look at it.

If it is off the vertical, to either the right or left, then you have rolled your wrists through the ball either at or after impact.

If the leading edge is off the vertical to the left, the hands have rolled the face into the closed position. If it is off the vertical to the right, the hands have opened the face. Make sure that you keep the club-face square in relation to your body all the way through your swing.

First drop the hands to about waist high. Then make this check ...

Here are six golfers in the same position. The pictures don't look exactly the same because they were taken from different angles but, trust us, they are. Make sure you check your club-face at the end of each shot.

At the finish of every shot, the club-face should still be square. The leading edge should be vertical.

Why should you be concerned about what happens to the club-face after impact with the ball? The answer is simply that if the face is coming out of alignment after the impact, it is only a matter of time before it happens before the impact. Errors of face alignment at or after impact will affect accuracy, sometimes with disastrous results.

Remember the face must be square at the finish. If it is coming out of alignment, you must discover where and when in your swing to correct it.

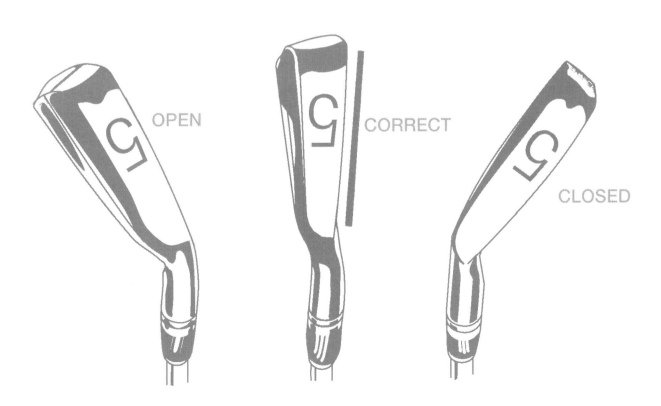

OPEN

CORRECT

CLOSED

How not to do it

Most golfers have no idea what should happen during the follow-through. Most players and even some teachers regard the follow-through as an afterthought. It is not; it is one third of the swing.

Remember it is not enough just to hit the ball. The ball must be 'driven forward'. To do this, your hands and arms must be trained to maintain a straight line beyond impact through to a quarter, half, three-quarter and full finish. Your body should play a vital role in achieving this because it is the turn of your body, hips and legs that will allow your hands and arms to swing unrestrictedly through the long swing apex to end in a balanced finish.

Here are some first-time visitors to the Swing Factory showing us how not to do it. Make sure you are not making the same mistakes.

TV star   Aristocrat   Skier

Admiral   Communicator   Philosopher

PR consultant   Estate agent   Socialite

'Whether you think you can or you can't, you are usually right'
HENRY FORD

swing & tempo

The swing – the whole master sequence from start to finish

Stage 1

Your hands and arms intiate the takeaway and have control of the club at all times. Your knees stay flexed throughout the backswing, supporting the turn of your shoulders and hips.

At halfway back, a line drawn down the shaft would point between the feet and the ball; the club-face is square in relation to the body.

Stage 2

At the top of your backswing, the shoulders are turned 90 degrees and your hips are turned 45 degrees. Your body has maintained a constant height, with your left arm free from the body and opposite your right shoulder. Your wrist break is maintained.

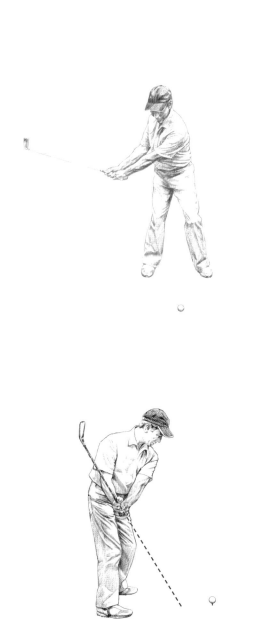

Stage 3

As your hands and arms start the downswing, your weight immediately moves to your left foot. Halfway down, your hips have returned to the same position as they were in at the address.

From halfway down, your right hand delivers the club-head to the ball. At impact, your hips have turned through 45 degrees and your shoulders should be square or slightly open.

Stage 4

Your hips turn fully through the quarter, half and three-quarter finishes with the club-face square in relation to your body. At the three-quarter finish, your hands and arms are opposite your left shoulder, your left leg is straight and your right knee is almost touching your left leg. Your right foot is up on the toe.

Tempo
The key to the consistent swing – how to remember everything that you have learned

Finding the correct tempo to your swing will give it the final polish. In fact, when you get your tempo right, you will realise that it enables you to remember everything that you have learned about the swing in this book, because tempo is the master regulator of the entire system. The right tempo enables the sequence of the swing to occur in the correct order with perfect timing. And all this happens automatically when you have built tempo into your swing.

Tempo is acquired by training. You have to condition yourself to perform the swing action that you have learned at the same tempo no matter what the conditions are, even in driving wind and rain. This conditioning process will then take over from your reflex or subconscious instinct to develop power before it is required. This instinctive reaction ruins timing and swing shape. Tempo not only brings these unruly impulses under control, it actually negates them altogether.

Where do these reflex actions come from? The answer is that it is your eyes that stimulate these powerful reflexes. Unlike many other sports, such as tennis, cricket or football, in golf you have a lot of time visually to assess your shot. You consider the distance and power required, the wind, the slope, and the lie.

When you add all this up, you can easily make the mistake of allowing the idea of power to dominate your thinking. In fact, the chances are that even when you are playing your shot, your mind is on the target area rather than the job in hand. Your sequence of priorities is wrong and so, consequently, is the sequence of your swing.

To do it right, you have to do it differently. You have to consider your problem calmly, assessing power and distance. But your acquired sense of tempo gives you a feeling of where in the swing sequence that power will be developed. And you should be confident that you know that your controlled swing action will produce the required power at the right time. That is, maximum club-head acceleration will occur at and through the ball in each and every one of your swings. This will give you uniform power and distance for every club in the bag. So, having assessed your shot and selected your club, your tempo guarantees that power is developed in the right place in the sequence, making for a shot of predictable length.

When you lift your head up in the swing or look up before the ball has been struck, it is a reflex. It happens because you have released power too early, so you look up to see the result.

You should never do this. Your eyes remain on the ball, awaiting the release of power that occurs between your feet. It is not a conscious action. You are still looking at the ball because power has not yet been released. When it is released at the right place, you look up – a logical sequence of events. Hence the expression 'hit early … look early, hit late … look late'.

So tempo is the ultimate refinement that concentrates power at exactly the right place every time you swing.

Tempo is a matter of establishing the speed of the hand and arm swing that allows enough time for a smooth transition from your backswing to your downswing. You have to learn how to swing down into the ball, allowing yourself sufficient time to release power with the hands and wrists at the correct moment.

Why is this so important? Because you have to retain the shape of your swing. Only by retaining a constant tempo can you keep a constant swing shape. Tempo and swing shape are indivisible. If you distort your tempo, then your swing shape will vary and vice versa.

What is more, if your tempo varies, your release point with the hands will also vary. This will result in erratic length and inaccuracy; in a word: inconsistency.

Most golfers swing much too fast to retain control over the delivery, so their point of release and the shape of their swings are subject to constant variation. You cannot standardise the shape of your swing and point of delivery until you have a constant tempo.

Tempo makes the difference between golf champions and the rest of the pack. Tempo makes a player feel powerful. He senses that he has the time and the control to develop maximum power to the ball. Tempo alone creates this mechanical excellence, which lasts through season after season, never varying.

Exercise A
Tempo

To help you find the right tempo, here is an exercise to work with. You might find this exercise helpful before you go out to play to make sure you don't swing too fast. Assume the correct address position with both arms extended and the palms of your hands facing each other. The distance between your hands should be equal to the width of your shoulders. Now simply move both arms up together to just above head height and down again. Repeat this up and down motion first without and then with a club in your hands.

The speed at which you move your arms in this exercise is the speed at which you should swing your hands and arms in the golf swing itself.

Note how smooth and easy this up and down action is. No effort is required. It is a genuine swing of the hands and arms. This smoothness and freedom must be carried over to your golf swing. You must discipline yourself to swing the club at this speed in your golf swing.

Some words of warning as you practise this exercise. Keep your height constant. Do not allow your body to rise up as your arms swing up. If you do, you are not swinging your arms, you are moving the arms by lifting the body, just as players do in a bad takeaway. Once you have stabilised your height, guard against breaking your wrists to move the club. You must swing your arms from the shoulders. Only then will genuine separation be achieved. Unless you can do this exercise, you cannot possibly achieve the swing model. Your arms must swing freely from the shoulder joints not from the wrists or elbows.

Remember, as your hands reach the top, they slow down. This is how it should be. This slowing down as the arms reach maximum leverage must also be achieved in the golf swing itself. It is the essence of timing and tempo.

Do this exercise often both to reinforce the sensation of separation and to establish the tempo of the swing.

'The way to develop self-confidence is to do the thing you fear and get a record of successful experiences behind you. Destiny is not a matter of chance, it is a matter of choice: it is not a thing to be waited for, it is a thing to be achieved'

WILLIAM JENNINGS BRYANT

summary

The beginner

'Great things are not done by impulse, but
by a series of small things brought together'
VINCENT VAN GOGH

Now that you've learned the shape of your swing, it is time to visit the driving range to work on your tempo and to learn how to deliver the ball to the target. Aim to hit a maximum of fifty balls and make sure that you take a practice swing between each shot and check the shape of it by breaking it down into the four positions that you have learned. At each position, check that the blade remains square and your hips are in the right position. When you complete your swing, hold your follow-through for a moment or two to remind yourself where you should be at the end of your swing.

Hit every ball off the tee. Don't be tempted to try to hit it directly off the mat. This will both build your confidence and stop you from leaning back to try to elevate the ball. Beginners often make this mistake and as a result fail to bring the club down properly on to the back of the ball. All you need to focus on is striking the ball with the middle of the blade and along the correct club-line. The rest will follow later. A good way to vary your shots is to practise with a variety of finishes. Start your first ten with a quarter finish, then your next ten with a half finish and then the same number with a three-quarter finish. Always hold your balance at the finish, bringing your arms to hip height and checking the blade angle.

This is a very important part of the swing model that helps you to build the correct finished shape of your swing. To keep your tempo right, try putting your club down between shots and swinging your arms gently to remind yourself of the perfect speed at which you should be swinging. Ideally, you should stay at the driving range until you can cleanly strike at least 50 per cent of your shots off the tee in the desired direction. Don't let your bad shots depress you. Even Tiger Woods hits bad shots. One of the secrets of his success is that he is able to let a bad shot go from his memory so he can concentrate on the next one.

This exercise will build your confidence and help you to understand just how relaxed you need to feel when you play a good golf shot. It will also mean that on your first visit to the course it won't humble you and drive you to despondency. Once you feel you've reached this level of competence, you can make your first visit to the course.

There can be nothing more intimidating than your first few visits to a golf course. Not only do you have to deal with the pressure of your first drive off the tee, but chances are that you will have a playing partner to worry about and even if there aren't a group of members standing

Forget your score, forget the bunkers, forget about playing from the rough, just keep returning to the fairway, teeing up your ball every time, and try again.

with a drink in their hand on the balcony watching you drive off, it will feel like there are.

I still have a framed photograph given to me by a friend who invited me to play at a charity golf day at St Andrews. It was to be only the third round of golf I had ever played and, despite my protestations of incompetence, he reassuringly insisted that there would be plenty of hack golfers coming and I should have nothing to fear.

On the seventh tee in preparation for a shotgun start stood a photographer capturing the completed swing of each player as a souvenir. Intimidated by all the possibilities of a mis-hit drive, I watched with increasing nervousness as all three of my playing partners calmly pulled their drivers from their bags and launched their golf balls up the middle of the fairway to the accompanying click of the camera. Not wanting to be left out, I ambitiously left my 5-iron in the bag and reached for my driver – not a club I was familiar with. My framed photograph of the result still holds pride of place in my study. I have completed a rather extreme follow-through, taking the tee and some turf with me; the eyes of the casual spectators captured in shot behind me are searching down the fairway in expectation, but the ball sadly remains firmly planted on the grass in front of my left foot.

There is no cure for inexperience, but you can make it easier for yourself. When you first play on a course you should give yourself a chance of enjoying it by sticking to the following rules. Take a 5-iron off the first tee. Leave the harder clubs to hit in your bag. Always tee up your shots on the tee and the fairway. If you hit your ball in the rough, in a bunker or anywhere tricky, pick the ball up and go back to the fairway with a tee

and carry on. It is important to get the feeling of hitting the ball well. Don't try to master the harder parts too soon. The more confidence you can give yourself, the better.

Remember your swing has been built to last a lifetime and, like a fine wine, it will improve with age, but to begin with you will be vulnerable, particularly if you make life too hard for yourself. See your swing as something delicate and fragile, requiring careful nurturing. It has, after all, been constructed in easily defined shapes and now, little by little, you have added the tempo and power. But remember with a new swing the structure can be perfect but the margin of error can be small. The face of the club must be square to the ball at the right depth with extraordinary precision at speed, and it has to be moving on the intended line of flight. A tiny fraction out and you will be in trouble, hence the emphasis in this book on acquiring precision in your swing. Fail in this and you will fail in everything from a golfing point of view. And when things go wrong in golf, you will find it easy, if you are not careful, to let your confidence drop and for things to get worse rapidly.

Once on the golf course, the priority is to learn to strike the ball cleanly. Forget your score, forget the bunkers, forget about playing from the rough, just keep returning to the fairway, teeing up your ball every time, and try again. In time you won't even have to try. Allow yourself four full shots on every hole and two putts. After that, go to the next tee and wipe the last hole from your mind. For the first three months or so, this is the way you should play golf.

Don't be unnerved on the first tee. It is the most nerve-racking moment in golf. Remember all those blue-blazered, confident voices in the bar

started once upon a time too. They, too, have completely missed the ball, shanked it into someone's garden, or generally made a fool of themselves on the golf course, so don't let their presence get you down. Playing golf is a bit like driving a car: once you get out there on your own, you get better very quickly. In a few weeks you will find you have come on a very long way. You will have made a beginning and you will now have a blueprint to follow if things go wrong. Stick with the four simple shapes that are required of a good player and you will find that you can deliver the club-head on to the ball with a great deal of precision. With time and patience, you will find that you have a swing that will enable you to play the best golf that you are capable of playing.

A final warning: every golfer wants to get better and better. That is the nature of the game's addictiveness. But be careful because it is very easy to destroy what you have built by tinkering. A round with a good player or a professional can often lead to suggestions about how to get that extra distance for your shots, or how to keep the ball low on a windy day. Don't let anyone interfere with what you have so patiently built. Many good swings are ruined by some well-intentioned advice, and another person's golfing dreams come crashing down to earth.

Resist the trap and don't let other people's tips destroy what you have. Just stick with your game plan and return to the blueprint if you begin to struggle.

A course summary

You should now have the foundations of the perfect swing. You should understand what should happen at each and every point in your swing and you should have an idea of where and when you are going wrong and how to correct it.

One thing you can be sure of: this method works. This analysis of the golf swing and the teaching method that it is based upon produces better golfers.

There are no gimmicks, no cures for hooks and slices. If you habitually hook or slice, you can be sure that there is something fundamentally wrong with your swing. There is no point in being given a cure for your slice that will ultimately become a hook. So if you want to play good, rewarding golf, you must have a sound method. And that is what this book should have given you.

The true measure of a golfer's ability is the quality of his worst shots. What you will gain from the method you have learned is that it will make your worst shots less punitive.

And let's face it. The essence of success in any sport is that your minimum standard of performance is extremely high. In golf this is quite impossible without a sound, consistent swing.

When tournament professionals come to the Swing Factory for tuition, Steve Gould and D. J. Wilkinson are not impressed by their best shots. It is their worst shots that they are interested in. These are the shots that will ruin their scores and put them out of the running on payday.

In order to score well consistently, you must have a sound action. Then your worst shots will only be marginally off line. If you practise the method as often as you can, you will find that you can produce respectable scores all the time. And that, after all, is what most golfers dream of.

There has been little mention of the short game in this book; only that the half swing is the foundation for all your chipping and wedge play. The art of chipping and putting, and the many other complexities of the long and short game could take up books in themselves. For the moment, we hope this book will change your golfing life and give you years of golfing pleasure.

212

If you practise the method as often as you can, you will find that you can produce respectable scores all the time. And that, after all, is what most golfers dream of.